2/04

3000 800055 49077
St. Louis Community College

Meramec Library
St. Louis Community College
11333 Big Bend Blvd.
Kirkwood, MO 63122-5799
314-984-7797

D1309604

WITHDRAWN

St. Louis Community College
at Meramec
Library

Klaus Reichold

# PALACES

## THAT CHANGED THE WORLD

PRESTEL

Munich · Berlin · London · New York

# CONTENTS

# FOREWORD

Many palaces, and royal residences have emerged seemingly unscathed from the vicissitudes of time. Their facades gleam immaculately, and inside, the gilding appears to have been applied just yesterday. In many other historic buildings, however, when one steps through an ancient door, when a threadbare brocade or table service with obvious signs of wear strikes our eye, the past seems to come alive. It is like being in the theater. The curtain rises to reveal people going about their everyday lives at a royal court, involving themselves in the political affairs, or planning the battles that will later go down in history—a vision of human greatness and failings, triumphs and tragedies. For what were palaces, royal castles, and residences if not stages on which the history of the world was played out, with the script being continually rewritten and constant changes made to the costumes and scenery.

This is architecture that has witnessed the actions of celebrated monarchs and despised despots, has been the scene of opulent receptions and exquisite balls, family dramas and war council meetings. The walls reverberate with the voices of wise rulers and the intrigue of courtiers, the sounds of passion and murder, and the denizens of these fabulous places cannot always be counted among the fortunate. Take P'u-i, for example, the last emperor of China, who complained about the "unprecedented obsession with ceremony" that oppressed him in his Beijing palace and recalled: "In this tiny corner of the world I spent the most absurd childhood imaginable."

The famous Empress Elizabeth of Austria, named "Sisi," also felt constricted by the rigors of court etiquette. She fled the Vienna Hofburg as often as she could, traveling for months on end and not even returning home for Christmas celebrations—for fear of her dominating mother-in-law, who was the true power behind the throne. No more pleasant was life for the doges of Venice. As soon as their coronation was over they became little more than "slaves of the republic," being expected to function perfectly and accept a broad curtailment of their personal rights without demur.

Elsewhere, admittedly, rulers threw all inhibitions to the winds. Grand Duke Cosimo II de'Medici reputedly transformed the Palazzo Pitti into a den of dwarves and tipplers whose noisy nocturnal revels were the talk of the town. Occasionally, even the last moral bastions fell. Pope Alexander VI, temporary master of the Vatican palace, was once described as "the most successful incarnation of the devil on earth" by the French author, Stendhal. In fact, it would be hard to name a crime that was not committed by him or one in which he was not involved.

Impishness was shown by the Japanese emperor who received the German traveler, Engelbert Kaempfer, at an audience in the year 1692. Evidently overcome with boredom, the emperor ordered his European guests to "walk back and forth, then dance, imitate a drunken man, stammer Japanese, paint, read in Dutch and German—and sing," before taking leave of them with great obeisance. Hard-headedness was a trait shared by many rulers. Louis XIV of France, for example, is known to have impatiently dismissed any complaint about the shortcomings of Versailles. Court officials protested about their constricted living quarters under the roof—the immense height of the staterooms made them impossible to heat and the incessant drafts were sure to ruin everybody's health sooner or later. But the Sun King refused to have any changes made, fearing they would impair his aesthetic experience of the palace.

Ludwig II, the Bavarian fairy-tale king, went one step farther. He is said to have wanted his castle, Neuschwanstein, demolished after his death, to prevent his private apartments from being "desecrated and defiled by plebeian curiosity." The order—if it was ever given—was fortunately never carried out.

The present volume is not a scholarly compendium on the history of the construction and furnishing of palaces, royal castles, and residences. Rather, it is a book of illustrations and essays that relate just a few of the anecdotes and episodes from the rich and fascinating tales spun around these historically and architecturally fascinating palaces scattered around the world. With the exception of Berlin City Palace, which was completely demolished in 1950, all of the buildings presented here are accessible to visitors, at least in part or on certain days. Step across the threshold into these palaces, royal castles, and residences and stride out across the World Stage.

*Klaus Reichold*

WINDSOR CASTLE
England, Windsor,
construction begun c. 1078

The five-hour coronation ceremony did not go off very smoothly. The Archbishop of Canterbury, congenitally absent-minded, put her signet ring on the wrong finger, and removing it later was a painful procedure. The imperial orb was presented to her much too early in the ceremony. Then the ancient Lord Rolle stumbled before the throne and had to be helped back to his feet, before he could do her majesty his honors. Yet, the nineteen-year-old Victoria (1819–1901) took it in her stride—as indeed her whole reign was to be singularly untroubled.

She absolutely enjoyed her independence. Queen Victoria's first official act was to have her bed removed from her mother's room, ending what had long become a bothersome sleeping arrangement. Yet she still felt oppressed by having too many people around her giving

> Having arrived at Windsor, we immediately went to our chambers. Albert had put on his Windsor jacket, sat me on his knees, kissed me and was so kind and tender. The rest of the evening I spent on the sofa, because I had a headache. Albert consoled me. He gave me tender names that I had never heard before. What bliss!
>
> Based on an entry in Queen Victoria's diary, February 10, 1840

her unwanted advice. So she began to leave London all the more frequently, especially after marrying her cousin, Prince Albert of Saxe-Coburg-Gotha in 1940. Albert, too, took as little pleasure in the hurly-burly of the capital as Victoria, and they both enjoyed country life and their private bliss all the more.

The couple's home of preference became Windsor Castle, the hereditary residence of the eponymous English royal house, located about thirty-five kilometers west of London. It was within these venerable walls that Victoria had brashly asked for Albert's hand. Now, at Windsor, with her beloved spouse beside her, began the happi-

2

est days of her life. Nine children issued from their marriage, which was soon lauded as one of the great love stories of the nineteenth century.

Yet Albert was not only Victoria's fairy-tale prince, but also the "secret king." On the eighteenth anniversary of her wedding, in 1858, she reportedly said that her marriage was a blessing for everyone in the country, with Albert having made the monarchy more popular with the people than ever before. Yet the couple would be granted only three more years together. On December 14, 1861, completely overworked, Albert died of typhoid at the age of forty-two.

Victoria's passionate love gave way to a deep mourning. The room in the eastern tract of the Upper Ward at Windsor where Albert had died was to remain untouched, and the queen could not sleep unless she had Albert's nightshirt alongside her. Victoria retired almost completely from public affairs, bowed despite her great self-confidence to a parliamentary government, and by so doing, helped the English middle class to an unprecedented burgeoning. Nonetheless, she was never able entirely to overcome her loss.

For the rest of her life Victoria wore widow's black, and commemorated her love by establishing the Royal Albert Hall and the Victoria and Albert Museum in London. At the Lower Ward of Windsor Castle, she had the sepulchral chapel once planned for Henry VII, converted into the Albert Memorial Chapel, and in Frogmore, built an elaborate mausoleum, where Albert found his last resting place. Victoria desired to be buried alongside him. This wish on the part of the "Mother of the Empire" was fulfilled when, after sixty-four years of rule, she died on January 22, 1901, taking an entire era along with her to the grave.

Nostalgia has since idealized the Victorian era into a Golden Age. For Victoria herself, it may well have consisted of dark decades, whose true symbol was the widow's veil.

1   Prince Albert, Queen Victoria, and the royal family, 1857
2   *Queen Victoria in Coronation Robes*, painting by Sir George Hayter, 1838
3, 4 Windsor Castle is an official residence of the Queen and the largest inhabited castle in the world
5   The twin towers of the Norman Gate

3

4  5

# PRAGUE CASTLE   Prague

Many a contemporary of Rudolf II (1552–1612), Emperor of the Holy Roman Empire, thought him a weird fellow. They said this "eccentric in the Hradčany," as he later came to be known, was a great sorcerer and had made a pact with the devil. It was true that Rudolf II, perhaps more than any other ruler of the period, was intrigued by everything mysterious and occult. His belief in supernatural forces already came to the fore in the early summer of 1583, when after seven years of reigning in Vienna, he shifted his residence to Prague. The move was reputedly made on the advice of his astrologists, who viewed the city on the Vltava as a melting pot of magic wisdom.

*As possessions of His Most Serene Majesty, Emperor Rudolf II, at Prague Castle, are to be listed: a pair of rhinoceros horns with magic powers; iron nails that stem from Noah's Arc; a crocodile in a case; a soft fur which dropped from the sky into His Majesty's camp in Hungary; the teeth of a Siren from the Aegean Sea; a death's mask of yellow agate; a living pair of mandrakes…*

From the inventory of Rudolf II's cabinet of curiosities at the Hradčany, 1607–11

PRAGUE CASTLE
Czech Republic, Prague
Construction begun in the
ninth century

In fact, nothing at Rudolf's court was undertaken without his stargazers. They were consulted before every decision, and whoever wished an audience with him had first to submit his horoscope. The emperor was also an adept of alchemy. Masters of the art came from far and wide to Prague, in search of the biting fumes of hissing and foul-smelling concoctions of the *prima materia*, the original substance of all being, as Rudolf looked on starry-eyed. Their laboratories stretched all along the "Golden Lane" in the northeast section of Prague Castle hill, where Italian alchemists purportedly succeeded in

creating "84 hundredweights of gold and 60 hundredweights of silver."

Yet the emperor was not only interested in astrology and alchemy. In his apartments he received Jehuda Löw ben Bezalel, head of the Jewish community in Prague—ostensibly in order to question him about the Golem, an artificial creature mentioned in the Kabala, the early works of Jewish mysticism. Moreover, he discussed the medical effects of precious stones with healers, and consulted his court astronomers Tycho Brahe and Johannes Kepler about the calculation of the planets' orbits. Keen to unravel the riddles of the universe, Rudolf collected everything that might represent a building block of creation, from clay fragments covered with hieroglyphs to crystals and fossils, which were supposed to harbor natural forces that would be passed on to anyone who owned them.

The Hradčany, which its master's hobbies had made the cultural and intellectual center of the empire, became the most significant cabinet of curiosities in the entire Western world. Thanks to the countless orders Rudolf II placed with artisans, Prague developed into the renowned "Golden City." On the other hand, no funds

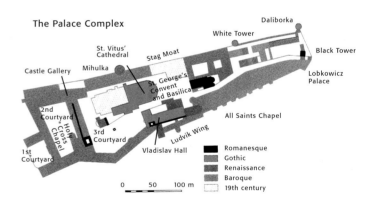

The Palace Complex

remained for a long-needed expansion of the old hereditary castle. The only significant buildings erected on Hradčany Hill during Rudolf II's reign were earmarked for his collections: the Gallery of Paintings and the Hall of Sculptures.

Finally his ambitious brother, Matthias (1557–1619), forced him to abdicate and ascended the throne. When Rudolf II died an embittered man four years later, his brother was quite fearful. On account of Rudolf's supposed magic powers, Matthias believed his brother had become a zombie who haunted the palace by night, awaiting an opportunity for revenge.

3

5

1 *View of Prague Castle*, engraving by Joris Hoefnagel, 1595
2 The "Golden Lane," which purportedly housed the alchemists' laboratories
3 Prague Castle seen from Charles Bridge
4 Zehetner's description of an imperial banquet in Prague, in 1585
5 Vladislav Hall, where court festivities and tournaments were hosted

4

## The Monarchy's Descent into Hell

# THE LOUVRE  Paris

THE LOUVRE
France, Paris, 1190–1870
Architects: Pierre Lescot,
Claude Perrault, Louis le Vau,
François d'Orbay, Charles
Lebrun, Jacques Lemercier,
et al.

French rulers never really loved the Louvre. Although its history extends back to the Middle Ages, it served as royal residence for no more than one hundred and fifty years—especially in the sixteenth and seventeenth centuries, when increasing pomp and circumstance required a suitable stage on which to unfold. Yet by the time of Louis XIV (1638–1715), the Louvre had again lost its function as seat of the monarchy. When the Sun King moved his court to Versailles, the abandoned tracts were taken over by the Royal Academy. The palatial rooms now housed artists at work, and under the roof lived scholars like the mathematician and astronomer Jean Sylvain Bailly, who had installed a little observatory in his study. The royal collections also remained in the Louvre, and were finally opened to the public—a demand on the part of the people, supported among others by the author Denis Diderot.

The first concrete suggestions for a "Central Museum of the Arts," however, were soon shelved. By the latter

*The date was November 18, 1793. In the palace of the deposed king the men of the revolution opened the "Central Museum of the Arts." They wished to give the people access to the accomplishments of civilization. For the progress of freedom is not only one of law but also one of culture. The accomplishments of civilization, the treasures of the artistic spirit, must be open to all men and women.*

François Mitterrand, in his *The Grand Louvre: History of a Project,* 1993

half of the eighteenth century certain tracts of the royal palace were in such a dilapidated state that a complete demolition of the Louvre was considered. And the citizens of the country had other worries: on July 14, 1789, the French Revolution broke out. As a result, Louis XVI was forced to return to the capital, for if he wished to remain in power, they said, he must rule the country

from Paris. The monarch had no choice. He moved into the Tuileries Palace, west of the Louvre. However, no preparations had been made. The building had stood empty for sixty-seven years. When they arrived there, the king's retinue was aghast: "Some slept on tables or benches, others managed to find cots. In the midst of this hopeless caravansary, Louis XVI, his spouse, and their children lived as if in a nightmare. They inspected the palace from top to bottom, ordered the necessary repairs, and had furniture brought from Versailles," one biographer recounts.

Yet the days of the monarchy were numbered. "Now the terror must penetrate into the palace, from which it has issued so many times," the people cried. On the night of August 9, 1792, the moment had come. Armed with stones, clubs, and rifles the revolutionary mob marched on the Louvre in order to put an end to the French monarchy. At the Tuileries, a bloodbath ensued. By noon the next day, over 2,000 people lay dead between the Champs-Elysées and the Louvre. Bourbon rule had come to an end in an apotheosis of horror. The king,

who had survived the carnage, was deposed and died under the guillotine.

But the Louvre survived the turmoil of those days. It was even restored and expanded. Even before the year of Louis XVI's death was out, the long-demanded "Central Museum of the Arts" was established. After all, said the spokesmen of the revolution, the treasures from the royal collections were "the most wonderful monuments to French genius" and perfectly suited to "furthering public education and reason." Today the Louvre counts among the richest museums in the entire world.

4

1  An altar painting from the fifteenth century depicting the Louvre
2  Louis XVI shortly before being beheaded, anonymous engraver
3  The Louvre by night with I.M. Pei's Glass Pyramid—now the entrance to the museum—in the center
4  *The Louvre at the Time of Napoleon II*, painting by Victor-Joseph Chavet, 1857

# THE HOFBURG   Vienna

When the court librarian looked out the window, he couldn't believe his eyes. Down in the courtyard of the Hofburg in Vienna, Francis II (1768–1835), the last Emperor of the Holy Roman Empire, was pushing the four-year-old successor to the throne in a wheelbarrow. Father and son were apparently enjoying themselves royally. Yet the court librarian—a learned and respected man—lost his temper. He threw open the window and hissed at the emperor that a ruler should "occupy himself in a more useful and dignified way." Not an hour later he received his discharge papers. The Habsburgers had no intention of letting anyone prevent them from enjoying

*The glow of over 8,000 wax candles illuminated the two largest halls of the Vienna Court Castle. All of the platforms were covered in velvet—here in the colors of red and gold, there in silver and blue. A third hall had been transformed into an orange grove. There were throne baldachins for the rulers and the powerful, buffets with the most delicious refreshments— and the orchestras played waltzes.*

Friedrich Anton Freiherr von Schönholz, describing a ball held during the Congress of Vienna, 1844

life. The empress was no exception, once acting the leading role in a play called *The Frightful Witch Megaera* on the Hofburg stage. Yet soon the clouds of the Napoleonic Wars began to gather on the horizon.

When French troops marched on Vienna in 1805, the Hofburg cellars were rapidly bricked up in order to protect the wine from the enemy. A year later, the old Central European order collapsed. Under Napoleon's pressure, Francis II relinquished the Roman-German imperial crown on August 6, 1806, and declared the Holy Roman

THE HOFBURG
Austria, Vienna
Construction begun in 1275

Empire defunct. But this did not put an end to the history of the Hofburg as a residence. Back in 1804, Francis II had proclaimed that, by virtue of his authority as Holy Roman Emperor, he permitted himself to become Emperor of Austria. Now he called himself "Francis the First, by the Grace of God Emperor of Austria, King of Hungary and Bohemia, Galicia, and Lodomeria, etcetera, etcetera."

Yet the war and the French occupation of Vienna had almost bankrupted the state. The long prepared grand plans to expand of the Hofburg remained on the shelf. Nevertheless, this "city within the city," which now looks back on a 700-year building history, and consists of eigh-

teen tracts with 2,600 rooms, experienced its heyday under Francis I. During the Congress of Vienna, held from 1814–15 to define a new European order after Napoleon's fall and chaired by the Austrian foreign minister Prince Clemens Wenzel von Metternich, dozens of crowned heads resided in the Hofburg's guest apartments. A total of two hundred representatives of various nations were involved in the negotiations—including exotic figures like the pasha of Vidin, in present-day Bulgaria, who appeared in caftan and turban. In the evening, emperors and kings, princes and dukes amused themselves at banquets, comedies, and shows of horsemanship. Balls and soirées followed one another in breathless succession—the Congress danced.

Francis I's favorite way of recuperating from the nightly revels was gardening. One day a stranger approached him and, assuming he was the gardener, quizzed him about the care and nurture of various plants, bushes, and trees. The emperor willingly replied, and with a chuckle pocketed the two pieces of silver the stranger gave him for his troubles.

1  Emperor Francis I's crown in the Hofburg's treasury
2  The Emperor's monument in the Hofburg's courtyard
3  Francis I in his coronation vestments
4  The Hofburg's entrance
5  Aerial view of the entire complex

18

4

5

# CHÂTEAU OF BLOIS   Blois

CHÂTEAU OF BLOIS
France, Blois, thirteenth to seventeenth century
Architects: Domenico da Cortona, François Mansart, et al.

The rumors were rampant about Catherine de Médicis (1519–89), the invariably black-clad widow of Henry II, King of France: she was a snake, cruel and unscrupulous; she surrounded herself with sorcerers, diviners, and intriguing Italian courtiers; she built hidden stairways and dark dungeons into her castles, and had countless secret chambers filled with daggers, jinxed amulets, and

> *Catherine de Médicis squandered her whole fortune on Blois. Even the gloomiest back exit is decorated with magnificent paintings, and those tasteful gildings, which Catherine brought from Italy, are to be found in the chambers even today. For the princesses of her house loved to invest in France's castles the money their ancestors acquired through trade and to mark the walls of the royal apartments with their riches.*
>
> Honoré de Balzac, *The Human Comedy*, 1842–48

poisons. An "arsenal of evil" was presumed to exist at the château, which, next to Paris, was the queen's favorite residence. The study there still contains the exquisite original wall paneling, which in fact provides food for thought. Several of the two hundred and thirty-seven carved wood panels open, as if by a ghostly hand, when one steps on a pedal concealed behind the wainscot. Catherine de Médicis doubtless used these secret recesses, perhaps for jewelry, works of art, or documents. Whether she truly hid poison and weapons here, however, is another question. Whatever is said about the temperamental, astrology-mad Florentine lady, she was a majestic and resolute person who for decades was the true ruler of France, and thus one of the most powerful women in Europe. She also made lasting contributions to her adopted country. Many of the things for which France is famous today go back to Catherine.

The daughter of one of the most cultivated dynasties in Europe, Catherine brought recipes to her new homeland, which revolutionized French cuisine. She introduced her subjects to the unfamiliar use of knife and fork, gave the ballet a solid place at the French court, had perfumes developed, and even set accents in fashion matters. But

she had enemies. They scoffed at her as a "foreigner" who, far from being of royal blood, stemmed from an "Italian shopkeepers' family." To this opposition, partly originating from the Protestant movement, Catherine replied with diplomacy, intrigues, and violence.

She is said to have instigated the bloody St. Bartholomew's Day Massacre, in which at least 5,000 Huguenots lost their lives. The Château of Blois, too, became the site of dramatic events. On the second floor, in the King's Chamber, the Duke de Guise, spokesman of the aristocratic opposition, was killed by an assassin on December 23, 1588. His body was cremated in one of the great fireplaces there. Still, it would seem unlikely that Catherine had a hand in the conspiracy. Obese and suffering from chronic bronchitis, she had spent that day in bed one floor above. A short time later, on the eve of Epiphany 1589, twelve days after the Duke de Guise's death, Catherine de Médicis died of pneumonia.

The derision of her opponents followed her beyond the grave. As we read in the memoirs of a contemporary, "After she passed away, they did not speak about her much more than about a dead goat."

1 The loggia facade built from 1515 to 1524
2 Jacques Androuet Du Cerceau, the Château of Blois and its gardens, from *Les plus excellents bastiments de France*, 1579
3 View of Catherine de Médicis' study
4 The château's central stair-tower

4 >

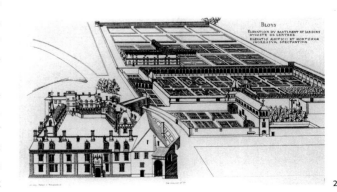

1   3

2

ALHAMBRA
Spain, Granada, 1300–54
Begun under Muhammad III,
Sultan of Granada; remodeled
under Yūsuf I from 1333–54

The American author Washington Irving (1783–1859) could not help but feel uneasy. He had been warned of the dubious characters who occupied the long abandoned, partly ruined apartments of the Alhambra. He was also familiar with the legend that the builder of this former royal palace high above Granada was a great sorcerer who sold his soul to the devil. Ever since, the fate of the Alhambra rested in the hands of the Prince of Darkness, who could turn his thumbs down at any time, bringing the once-glorious edifice down and burying whoever happened to be there. Yet Irving remained undaunted. For as his French fellow-writer François René de Chateaubriand had noted on the occasion of a visit to Granada in 1807, despite its dilapidated state the Alhambra was a "fairy-tale, sheer magic, glory, love."

So in 1829, Irving walked up the supposedly cursed driveway and passed through the gate. He arrived in one piece—and was overwhelmed. "No part of the edifice gives a more complete idea of its original beauty than this," he wrote of the Lion's Court, "for none has suffered so little from the ravages of time. In the center stands the fountain famous in song and story. The alabaster basins still shed their diamond drops," as they had at the time of the Moorish kings.

Being a literary man, Irving saw not only a masterpiece of Islamic architecture in the Alhambra but a sight steeped in history. He recorded all the legends and anecdotes relating to it he could find, and published them under the title *The Alhambra*. This two-volume work, which included a description of the execution of thirty-six cavaliers in a side wing of Lion's Court, became a best-selling travel book, woke the Alhambra from its centuries-long slumbers, and turned Granada into a focus of international tourism. What contemporary visitors can only dream of was vouchsafed to Irving, who during his researches was permitted to spend several weeks in the abandoned apartments of the palace. What we would grudge him less was his experience there. Alone in the Alhambra in the dead of night, Irving was haunted by the ghosts he had invoked. Hearing mournful sounds and screams, deep sighs and furious shrieks, he knew the thirty-six dead cavaliers had returned. Only when the early-morning sun awakened him the next morning did his surroundings reappear in their full beauty and glory, and he could hardly remember the oppressive dream of the night before.

*The peculiar charm of this old dreamy palace, is its power of calling up vague reveries and picturings of the past, and thus clothing naked realities with the illusions of the memory and the imagination. As I delighted to walk in the "vain shadows," I am prone to seek those parts of the Alhambra which are most favourable to this phantasmagoria of the mind.*

Washington Irving, *The Alhambra*, 1832

1 The Alhambra with the snow-covered foothills of the Sierra Nevada in the background
2 The Alhambra fell into disrepair in the eighteenth century. Engraving from the nineteenth century
3 The Lion's Court, the main residence of the sultans

1

2

# DOGE'S PALACE   Venice

For centuries Venice was a world power, "rich in gold, but richer still in reputation and name," as the poet Francesco Petrarch noted. One reason for this was a flourishing trade: "Exquisite goods from all countries of the world circulate in this superb city like the jets springing from the fountains," wrote one observer as early as 1267. At the same time, Venice commanded the largest fleet of war vessels in the Western world. Her galleys manned by thousands of seamen and soldiers ensured the security of Venetian merchants throughout the Mediterranean region—whether in the harbors or on the trade routes between Orient and Occident. As if effortlessly, Venetian troops conquered Dalmatia, Istria, Crete, Cyprus, and the Peloponnesus, not to mention nearly

*The Doge's Palace is indeed a remarkable edifice, but one whose exterior already clearly indicates that a duke of Venice is no prince who gives free rein to his whims and pleasures but the highest official of a stern, strict republic which merely puts these halls at his disposal, as another city would assign the third floor of their town hall to the mayor as official residence.*

Joseph Victor von Scheffel, *Memorial of Tobolino*, 1855

half of the Byzantine Empire. Finally the republic even expanded into its own hinterland and incorporated almost the entire area of today's northern Italy.

All of the threads of the empire came together at the Palazzo Ducale, or Doge's Palace, that magnificent building of which the French philosopher Hippolyte Taine said that, against the backdrop of the city on the lagoon,

it recalled "a unique diamond in the center of a piece of jewelry." Yet the doge, the ruler of the Republics of Venice and Genoa who was chosen for life, struck his contemporaries as being a "poor dog." Not even his opulent apartments in the east wing could mitigate this impression, for it was the merchants who had the say. They reached their decisions in the Hall of the Grand Council, the imposing heart of the palace, which could accommodate up to 2,000. As early as 1506, these representatives already envisaged a world-changing project that would not be realized until the nineteenth century, the building of the Suez Canal.

The doges tended to stand at the margins during such consultations. For they were "not the lords but the honor-laden slaves of the Republic," as Petrarch noted. To that extent their grand palace with its colonnaded substructure and surmounting marble block, a veritable symbol of the "city built on piles," may well have seemed more like a penitentiary than a residence to them. For as soon as they had taken their oath of office on the top step of the Giant Stairway in the courtyard of the palazzo, they entered on a life of privations. The doges were permitted to leave the palace only on official business, and their mail was monitored. They were forbidden to participate in commercial undertakings, to receive private visits, and to accept gifts—with the exception of flowers, aromatic herbs, and rose water.

"When I was elected, I was overcome by such a feeling of anxiety that I hardly knew what I was doing," confessed Ludovico Manin, the 120th doge of the republic. It was during his reign that the world power of Venice finally collapsed. When Napoleon appeared with his troops outside the city in 1797, Manin, appearing before the Grand Council in the hall of that name, returned his ducal cap and uttered the memorable words, "Well, this will not be needed any more." Whether the council suspected that this meeting would be their last, was not apparent from its members' faces. It was carnival season, and most of the gentlemen were wearing masks.

DOGE'S PALACE
Italy, Venice, c. 1350–1550
Architects: Filippo Calendario,
Giovanni and Bartolomeo
Bon, Antonio Rizzo, et al.

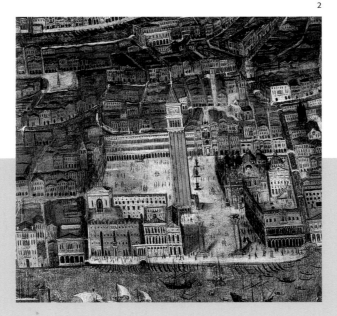

4

1  *Venice: The Doge's Palace and the Molo*,
   painting by Francesco Guardi, *c.* 1770
2  Piazza of San Marco, detail from a painting of Venice by G.B. Arzenti
3  *Doge Leonardo Loredan*, painting by
   Giovanni Bellini, *c.* 1501
4  View of the Doge's Palace
5  The Giant Stairway, named after the two
   colossal statues of Mars and Neptune
   embellishing it

5

# IMPERIAL PALACE   Beijing

The three-year-old P'u-i (1906–67), red in the face from crying, kicked and screamed, "I want to go home!" It took some effort to keep the lively boy from running away. Strong arms pressed him back onto the gold-embroidered cushion of his magnificent throne. "Then began the filing past of dignitaries. One after another they paid me their respects, with the prescribed three bows and nine *kotows*. Yet the longer the ceremony lasted, the more noticeable became my vehement protest," recalled P'u-i in his memoirs. But it was no use, and the hours of his enthronement dragged on. P'u-i finally became emperor of China, and lord over the Forbidden City.

The enormous palace complex surrounded by seven-meter-high walls at the heart of Beijing—a city within the

*Nowhere do ceremonies take such a dignified and solemn form as in the Forbidden City in Beijing. In a lofty hall supported by red columns where the daylight glare is screened by blue hangings, the youthful emperor sits enthroned like an idol. He is surrounded by great peacock fans, bronze vases, lion figures, and great bowls full of aromatic apples. The impression is so exotic that one entirely forgets the immense crowd of courtiers in the background.*

Gerhard von Mutius, German ambassador to Beijing, in a letter of May 16, 1908

IMPERIAL PALACE
China, Beijing
Construction begun c. 1300,
majorly revamped in the
seventeeth century

city populated by up to 20,000 officials and servants—was accessible only to members of the court. For the common people, the extensive grounds with their gateways and palaces, fountains, squares, and ceremonial halls were taboo. According to ancient tradition, the residence and seat of government of the Chinese rulers was not only a center of earthly power, but the crystallization point of transcendental forces. The Forbidden City was believed to have been built on a divine plan, and to mirror the design of the cosmos. Its buildings were said to represent the earth, the heavens, and the stars. Yet the true midpoint of the universe was the emperor himself. He alone was capable of mediating between this life and the afterworld, above and below, yin and yang, and of ensuring social harmony by maintaining a strict divine order.

Yet when P'u-i ascended the throne, this order was threatened. Despite the fact that he grew up in complete isolation from the outside world, the little emperor behaved as unpredictably as any other youngster his age: "Every one of my steps was subject to court etiquette. Even when I wanted to go to the imperial gardens to play, I was accompanied by dozens of eunuchs with sunshades, teapots, cookie jars, and gilded cinnabar pills against the heat. The magnificent train moved silently, solemnly, and in strict hierarchical order. But woe to them if I started to run. Then the whole procession rushed and stumbled after me until the eunuchs began to gasp for breath and everything fell into hopeless confusion."

Nor did age mellow P'u-i's attitude to centuries-old protocol. To his court officials' displeasure he obtained a bicycle and ordered all the wooden thresholds in the doors of the palace sawn off because they hindered the practice of his new favorite sport. When he came of age, P'u-i insisted that a telephone be installed in the palace. The court officials concluded that he had "lost the inviolable dignity of the Son of Heaven," and anticipated his downfall.

It came on November 5, 1924. P'u-i, the last emperor of China, was driven from his palace by the revolutionary movement. Although he missed the luxury, he was finally rid of bothersome ceremony. Before he died as a common citizen of Beijing in 1967, P'u-i said that, in contrast to the period he had spent on the imperial throne, he now felt like a free man.

1   Gate of Divine Pride
2   Pavilion of Imperial Peace
3   Imperial Garden
4   Gate of Earthly Tranquility
5   Six Western Palaces
6   Palace of Earthly Tranquility
7   Hall of Union
8   Palace of Heavenly Purity
9   Palace of the Culture of the Mind
10  Gate Of Heavenly Purity
11  Palace of Peace and Longevity
12  Hall of Preserved Harmony
13  Hall of Perfect Harmony
14  Hall of Supreme Harmony
15  Gate of Supreme Harmony
16  Meridian Gate

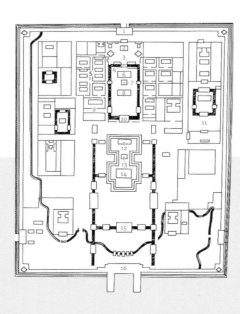

1   The six-year-old emperor P'u-i
2   View of the Forbidden City
3   The Halls of Harmony stand on a three-tier marble terrace
4   The throne in the Hall of Preserved Harmony, where the Emperor sat during official ceremonies

2

3  4

# CITY PALACE  Berlin

1

The entire palace was crammed with crates. Elaborate clocks and table centerpieces, tapestries and paintings, armchairs and secretaries—everything but the woodwork had been packed and prepared for evacuation. Berlin was anticipating the worst retaliation since Germany's attack on Poland on September 1, 1939, triggering World War II: bombardment from the air. It came in the early hours of February 3, 1945, over 1,500 heavy bombers mounted the most devastating raid yet on the capital of the Reich. The sky over Berlin was transformed into a roaring inferno. The palace, too, was gutted.

Although its interiors were largely destroyed, the massive walls, meters thick, withstood the heat. As a profes-

> By order of the communist regime, Berlin City Palace was dynamited on Thursday morning. With this act—and for no practical reason—the loveliest secular building in Berlin has been destroyed.
>
> The Berlin daily *Der Tagesspiegel*, September 8, 1950

sor of art history at Berlin's Humboldt University noted as late as August 1950, the palace stood there "in ruins—still of a fascinating massiveness and monumentality, a representative specimen of the specifically Northern German Baroque, worthy to stand side by side with St. Peter's in Rome and the Louvre in Paris."

By then, alas, the demolition of the impressive torso had long been decided on. According to a position paper issued by the East German communist regime, the City Palace was a symbol of imperialism, the Junker squire-archy, and serfdom, and stood in the way of planning for the new capital of the G.D.R. The public outcry was enormous.

Berliners, both east and west, recalled the checkered history of the former royal residence, which had witnessed so much since its inauguration in 1451: the rise of the electors of Brandenburg to kings of Prussia and emperors of Germany; the magnificent annexes designed by renowned Baroque architects Andreas Schlüter and Johann Friedrich Eosander von Göthe; Kaiser Wilhelm II's proclamation of World War I and his abdication at its end. And—under the Nazi regime—the notorious Reich Chamber of Visual Art, and the witch-hunt it launched from this site against "degenerate art." All of these memories were now to be wiped off the slate, irrevocably.

At three in the afternoon on December 30, 1950, the soaring dome collapsed with the last remnants of the palace into a tremendous cloud of dust. The site, over 23,000 square meters in area, was bulldozed to form a parade ground, which soon degenerated into East Berlin's biggest parking lot. Not even the erection, in 1976, of the Palace of the Republic on the eastern half of the former palace site could conceal the fact that Berlin's center no longer had a face.

After German reunification, a heated debate arose over the future of the site. The issue was apparently decided on July 4, 2002, when the German Bundestag voted to reconstruct the palace.

**CITY PALACE**
Germany, Berlin, 1443–1852
Architects: Caspar Theyss,
Hans Räspel, Count Rochus
zu Lynar, Andreas Schlüter,
Johann Friedrich Eosander
von Göthe, Martin Heinrich
Böhme, August Stüler, Albert
Schadow, et al.

1  The Knights' Hall in the City Palace
2  Aerial photograph of Berlin's old town before 1945, with the palace in the center
3  The Prince Elector's bridge with the palace in the background, 1898
4  Mock-up of the City Palace erected in front of the Palace of the Republic, 1995
5  A model of the palace, the west front

2

3

4

5

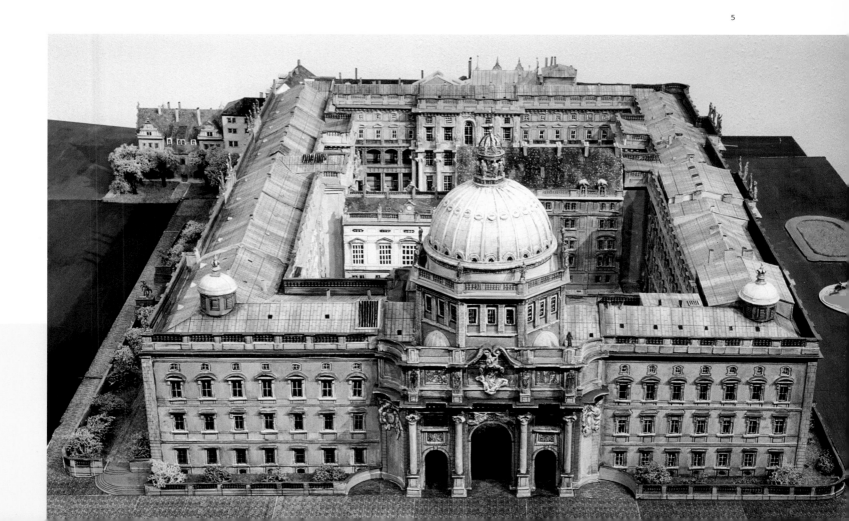

# VATICAN PALACE   Rome

Perhaps we would rather not have eavesdropped as the family council hatched their plots in the Borgia apartments, with which Pope Alexander VI (1431–1503) began the expansion of the Vatican Palace into the most magnificent residence of the sixteenth century. There was hardly a crime that he had not committed. The grandiose paintings covering the walls and ceilings give an idea of how this "most unholy of popes" saw himself—as an alchemist who could transform lead into gold, and as a reincarnation of Alexander the Great, who had once dreamed of world domination. The latter ambition would not be vouchsafed him. His plan to claim the Holy See as an hereditary office for his family was likewise thwarted. When, on June 29, 1500, the brand-new ceiling vault of the Sala dei Pontefici collapsed and nearly buried him under the rubble, it was considered a divine omen.

*There is no second place in Rome where one feels more spirited back into the Renaissance than at the Borgia apartments of the Vatican Palace. When the only thing to be heard by day is the tinkling of the fountain down in the courtyard, the people who spent their lives in these rooms suddenly come alive again: there Pope Alexander VI strides across the majolica floor in his brocade robes, there the sunlight plays over the blonde hair of his daughter, Lucrezia, there his son, Cesare, presents himself in gold-shimmering armor.*

Evelyn Marc Phillips, after the reopening of the Borgia apartments, 1897

It was the era of the Renaissance. Omnipotent rulers over the Vatican State, the popes reveled in the role of magnificent princes. Alexander VI stemmed from the dynasty of the Spanish Borgias, and due to his unscrupu-

VATICAN PALACE
Italy, Rome, 1450–1822
Architects: Antonio da
Firenze, Bernardo Rossellino,
Antonio Pollaiuolo, Donato
Bramante, Raphael, et al.

lousness he was looked upon as the greatest misfortune in papal history. The scandal had already begun with his election. Far from being based on the infusions of the Holy Spirit, it was the result of bribery. Hardly in St. Peter's chair, Alexander VI began to use his position like no other pope to shower offices and honors on members of his family, above all, his children. Despite his vow of celibacy, he had at least seven children by various women, and they openly frequented the Vatican. The Romans had long ceased to wonder about such goings-on. Innocent VIII, Alexander's predecessor, had been equally susceptible to the fair sex, and had married off his daughters with great pomp in the Vatican Palace.

At that period the deputies of Christ on earth had laissez-faire attitudes. They delegated the reading of the mass to their cardinals in order to enjoy a hunting spree or some other diversion. And when they did occasionally perform their spiritual duties, even a Corpus Christi Day procession could turn into a rollicking festival, as when Alexander VI, carrying the monstrance, was preceded through the streets of the Eternal City by fools beating tambourines.

In 1503, when the pope's death followed his moral one, the relief was great. Every memory of him was to be expunged. None of his successors wished to live in the Borgia chambers; the opulent rooms were entirely neglected, and for centuries thereafter used as storage spaces.

1   Portrait of Pope Alexander VI, engraving
2   Alexander VI's coat of arms in the Borgia apartments, by the artist Antonio da Viterbo, also known as Pastura, 1492–95
3   The Courtyard of the Pine Cone leading up to the Borgia apartments
4   View of the Vatican Palace

| 1 St. Peter's Square | 5 The Belvedere Courtyard |
| 2 St. Peter's Church | 6 Court of the Pine Cone |
| 3 Sistine Chapel | 7 Sacristy of St. Peter's |
| 4 Vatican Palace | 8 Teutonic Cemetery |

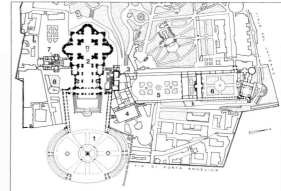

3

4

PALAZZO PITTI
Italy, Florence, 1457–1896
Architects: Luca Fancelli, Bartolomeo Ammannati, Alfonso and Giulio Parigi, Giuseppe Ruggieri, Gaspare Paoletti, et al.

Malicious tongues maintained the only reason he worked was to amass as large a fortune as he could and flaunt his wealth in people's faces. Admittedly, this had always been the best way to go down in the history of art. And the Florentine merchant, Luca Pitti, succeeded. The imposing residence on the left bank of the Arno that still bears his name, is one of the mightiest city palaces in Florence.

Friedrich Nietzsche found the building, continually expanded in the course of the centuries, so impressive that he declared it a perfect example of the "grand style." Even representatives of modern architecture like Ludwig Mies van der Rohe and Le Corbusier stood in awe of this facade and its cyclopean masonry. To other minds, Palazzo Pitti was merely repellent. It was "daunting" and "terrifying," they said, "the harshest and most forbidding

> *What a strange first afternoon it was that we spent in Florence! Going along the Arno we hurried to Trinity Bridge, and from there to Santo Spirito. Then suddenly, we stood in front of a colossal palace, and had no idea where we were. It was the Palazzo Pitti.*
>
> Jacob Burckhardt, *The Civilization of the Renaissance in Italy*, 1860

of all Florentine *palazzi*." Even the courtyard on the park side made "a rattling impression," which soon gave the visitor the feeling of "having put on chain mail armor."

Jacob Burckhardt, the eminent Swiss cultural historian, was likewise unable to make his peace with Palazzo Pitti. Its rigid monumentality, he stated, reflected what its contractor was—a man of power who despised the world. Indeed, Luca Pitti was considered extremely ambitious

and power-hungry. Especially his family's main rivals, the merchant dynasty of the Medici, were a thorn in his side. By building the palace he intended to relegate his competitors to the back seat and, initially, he succeeded. But when it became known that he had participated in a conspiracy against the Medici scion Piero the Gouty, Pitti lost his reputation—and his fortune. Over the following years the great palace fell into decay. Until 1549, when the Medicis, of all people, acquired it for the ridiculously small sum of 10,000 guilders.

Luca Pitti was no longer there to experience this indignity. Nor did he have to look on as his palace became, under Medici aegis, what he had always dreamed it would be: the social hub of the city and finally—once his rivals had risen to the rank of dukes and grand dukes of Tuscany—the splendid residence of a princely family that soon counted among the foremost in Europe. Pitti was also spared being witness to the opulent celebrations at which the Medici flooded the inner courtyard of the expanded palace and, on artificial waves, staged mock battles between magnificently decked-out galleys. Yet there was one thing that might have reconciled him to the fate of his family's former residence.

At Palazzo Pitti the destiny of his arch-rivals finally ran its course. Grand Duke Gian Gastone was the last male descendant of the long Medici line. He smoked, drank, gambled away his ancestral fortune, was considered insane, and reputedly spent his days at Palazzo Pitti among young male prostitutes, rogues and ne'er-do-wells. Seriously ill, he spent the last seven years of his life in bed, and died on July 9, 1737. "Sic transit gloria mundi," were reputedly his last words. "So goes the glory of the world"—Luca Pitti could certainly have subscribed to that.

1 Boboli Gardens and Palazzo Pitti before the Medici's extension, painting by Giusto Utens, c. 1600
2 Garden front of the palace in which Galileo Galilei was often a guest in later years
3 The "Sala dell'Iliade," the decoration from the nineteenth century
4 The imposing facade viewed from the Via Romana

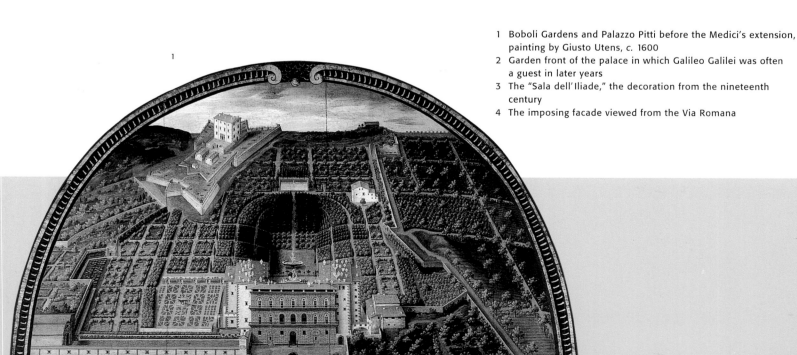

1

BELVEDER CON PITTI

2

3   4

# TOPKAPI PALACE    Istanbul

His titles included "King of Kings," "Shadow of God on Earth," and "Ruler over the White and Black Seas." The reigning Ottoman sultan was naturally lord over life and death as well, and not even court officials and ministers were spared his verdicts. Whoever fell out of the sultan's favor could count on being removed—by what means, the unfortunate could only speculate. Either they would receive a visit from the feared superintendent of the royal gardens, the sultan's traditional executioner, who always carried a thin strong cord and seldom left a delinquent's room without his head, or they inadvertently found themselves in the publicly accessible First Courtyard of Topkapı Palace. Here, the Executioners Fountain, where

*The sultan's palace is the first thing that strikes the eye of anyone who comes to Constantinople by sea. On the harbor side we are greeted by a pavilion on marble columns, where the exalted ruler is occasionally to be seen taking the air. On the other side, but likewise near the water, we can discern the window from which those who have been strangled in the palace by night are thrown into the sea.*

Jean Thevenot, *Travels in Europe*, Berlin, 1779

TOPKAPI, PALACE
Turkey, Istanbul, 1465–1840
Architects: Mimar Sinan, et al.

headsmen rinsed their swords and hands after doing their grisly job, still recalls the sudden end of countless dignitaries who, despite their rank, were executed alongside highwaymen and thieves.

Yet the ghosts of its murderous past pale in view of the opulent splendor of the most significant royal residence on Turkish soil. Topkapı Palace—seat of the Ottoman Empire for three hundred years—is justly praised as a unique "tent city in stone," whose pavilions adorned with

arabesques, elaborately tiled kiosks, bowers, harem, palace school, and freestanding buildings that house the library and royal collections, recall the nomadic origins of the Osmanlis. In its heyday, 40,000 members of the court and their servants lived within the palace walls—

a number the sultan found distinctly too high. As Ahmed III (1703–30) once declared, it was "quite unpleasant" to be surrounded by forty pages even "when I am putting on my trousers."

Topkapı was not only the hub of secular power, but a spiritual center as well. Its reliquary chamber contains highly revered Islamic relics: the cloak, personal seal and banner of the founder of the religion, Mohammad, and even several hairs from the Prophet's beard, one of his teeth, and a footprint. The treasury also harbors great valuables, such as the eighteenth-century dagger made world famous in 1964 by the movie thriller *Topkapi*. Missing, however, is a certain mechanical organ, which came to the Bosporus in 1599 as a gift from Queen Elizabeth I. The then sultan, Mehmed III, was so charmed by the sound of the instrument that he decided to retain the English organist whom the queen had sent along to demonstrate it. The musician, however, preferred to return home, reputedly fearing the loss of his head as soon as the sultan grew bored with his playing.

34

1  View from Topkapı Palace
2  The extensive palace complex
3  Reception at the court of Sultan Selim III (1789), painting attributed to Constantin Kapidagli
4  View over the roofs of the labyrinthine Topkapı Palace

# TEREM PALACE  Moscow

TEREM PALACE
Russia, Moscow, Kremlin,
1499–1636 (with nineteenth-
century additions)
Architects: Alevis Frjasin,
Antip Konstantinov, Bažen
Ogurcev, et al.

Mikhail Fyodorovich (1596–1645) was reputedly not very bright. They said he had trouble reading and writing, was uneducated, unambitious, and had no charisma, let alone vision. He was also considered shy and confused, but above all, too young. Nevertheless, at the age of barely sixteen, Mikhail Fyodorovich was elected czar by the diet and crowned in the Kremlin on July 11, 1613. It was a coolly calculated decision on the part of the representatives, since they expected that the young ruler's inadequacies would keep him from interfering in their grand political designs. They were not mistaken.

Mikhail Fyodorovich—the first ruler of the Romanov dynasty, which would reign until 1917—retired so completely into private affairs that later biographers would accuse him of a "veritably inglorious anonymity." Yet he still proved to be a lucky choice for the empire, for he was a lover of beauty and the arts. With Terem Palace, he commissioned the most magnificent architectural creation within the Kremlin walls, a fairy-tale residence that recalled the traditional Russian art of building in wood. Its roofs were covered with wrought iron, its windowpanes were made of mica, thin sheets of a transparent, opalescent, natural mineral.

Mikhail Fyodorovich lived in continual fear in his magnificent chambers. Only a few years previously, during the "Time of Troubles," one of his predecessors had been slain in the Kremlin, burned to ashes, stuffed into a cannon, and fired off in the direction of Poland, where he had originated. Yet Mikhail Fyodorovich really had no reason for anxiety. Never before were people in Russia able to express their opinion more freely, never before had they felt more united than under his reign. The country, beset by famine and uprisings, had grown calm and safe—and the arts flourished.

At the court of Mikhail Fyodorovich began the "Jeweled Age"—crowns, scepters, swords, saddles, cups, table decorations, bishop's mitres, book bindings, and liturgical accoutrements were so lavishly ornamented with gold, silver, pearls, and precious gems, that not even the glories of the Medicis could rival them. The czar's golden quiver alone was adorned with thirty-four sapphires, thirty-five rubies, one hundred and thirty-five emeralds, and one hundred and ninety-one diamonds. Mikhail Fyodorovich spent entire days among his goldsmiths and jewelers, who had their workshops on the lower floors of Terem Palace, discussing new designs with them.

This preoccupation is a likely explanation why he was so remiss in dealing with his subjects' wishes. At a certain hour, a box was lowered from his throne room window into the courtyard below, to receive people's petitions. Yet since the czar's reply was usually long in coming, they soon began speaking about "putting something in the long box"—a Russian idiom of which our equivalent would be, "to put something on the shelf."

*I have seen Moscow, this miraculous city, for only two days. And I thought I was in Asia: poverty and hovels even in the midst of the center, but interspersed with the glory of the palaces and gardens, the radiant domes of the churches and monasteries, and then the Kremlin with its resplendent facades, its golden gates, towers, and battlements. I could only goggle.*

Ernst Moritz Arndt, *Memoirs from the Outward Life*, 1840

The Kremlin

1  Cathedral Square
2  Cathedral of the Dormition
3  Cathedral of the Annunciation
4  Church of the Deposition of the Robe
5  Palace of the Facets
6  Cathedral of the Archangel Michael
7  Ivan the Great Bell Tower
8  Terem Palace
9  Church of St. Lazarus
10  Upper Cathedral of the Savior
11  Cathedral of The Twelve Apostles and Patriarch's Palace
12  Château de Plaisance
13  Arsenal buildings
14  Senate building
15  Great Kremlin Palace
16  Armory chamber
17  Buildings of the former Senate
18  Statue of Lenin
19  Congress Palace
20  Tomb of the Unknown Soldier
21  Obelisk
22  Alexander's Gardens
23  Great Stone Bridge
24  St. Basil's Cathedral
25  Lenin's Mausoleum
26  Red Square
27  Historical Museum
28  Revolution Square

2

1 The Czarist Jewels, fashioned in Terem Palace, 1627
2 View of the Kremlin
3 *The Election and Coronation of Czar Mikhail Fyodorovich*, 1856
4 Terem Palace from the inside
5 The facade of Terem Palace; "Terem" is the loft that originally served
  as a withdrawing room and bedroom. The name was later used to
  describe the whole building; in the center of the image is the window
  out of which a box was lowered to receive the people's petitions

3                                                    4          5

HOLYROODHOUSE
Scotland, Edinburgh,
1501–1681
Architect: Sir William Bruce of
Balkaskie, et al.

She did not really feel like celebrating. Not long since, she had lost her husband, King Francis II of France, who had been sickly since childhood. Now the eighteen-year-old widow, Mary Stuart (1542–87), was on a ship heading back to her homeland for, after all, she was Queen of Scots. Her people could hardly wait for the young monarch to arrive. When she set foot on Scottish soil in Leith harbor one dreary January morning in the year 1561, she was greeted at the dock by gay bonfires and an enormous crowd that accompanied her in a triumphal procession to Edinburgh. In the Scottish capital, French architects and stucco workers had been laboring to to the last minute to transform the palatial Holyroodhouse at the end of the Royal Mile into a jewel.

In earlier days, one could hardly see the forest for the trees on that site. This changed in 1128, when space was

*It was a truly infernal spectacle. Around five hundred Scotsmen who were convinced of their musical aptitude had gathered in front of the palace of Holyroodhouse, intending to serenade Mary Stuart with bagpipes, fiddles, and flutes. In fact, however, they played so off-tune that the queen feared she would lose her mind.*

Pierre de Bourdeille Seigneur de Brantôme, *Memoirs*, 1665–66

1 *Holyroodhouse*, a water-color by James Duffield Harding for Queen Victoria
2 A portrait of Mary Stuart, one of the most tragic figures in Scottish history
3 Memorial plaque for David Rizzio, who was murdered in Holyroodhouse
4 View of the courtyard
5 Holyroodhouse now houses the Scottish parliament

cleared for an abbey dedicated to the Holy Cross, or Holy Rood, to which a royal guest house was soon added. Expanded under James IV, Mary Stuart's grandfather, into a stately royal seat, Holyroodhouse soon became the social and cultural hub of the country, the "heart of Scotland."

The young queen moved into apartments on the first and second floor of today's northwest tower—but could not get a minute's sleep that night. Her faithful subjects kept fiddling and tootling under her windows into

the wee morning hours, their growing enthusiasm matched by growing dissonance, "so that Her Majesty's ears were just as offended as my own," as her French advisor Brantôme recalled in his memoirs. Yet this was not to be the only unpleasantness Mary Stuart was to face at Holyroodhouse.

On the evening of March 9, 1566, David Rizzio, the queen's charming Italian secretary, was arrested at the table where they were dining together, dragged through several chambers to the upper end of the main staircase, and killed with fifty-six dagger thrusts. The murderer—Mary's second husband, Lord Darnley, who believed Rizzio was his wife's lover—was not to live long himself. Barely a year after his bloody deed he was killed in an enormous detonation near Holyroodhouse, something of which Mary was reputedly not entirely innocent. She was forced to abdicate, spent the next nineteen years under house arrest in England, and on February 8, 1587, ended on the gallows of her royal rival, Elizabeth I, Queen of England.

Holyroodhouse began to fall into decay, a process accelerated by the uniting of Scotland and England into the empire of Great Britain in 1707. London was now the sole capital city. Still, the Stuarts' seat in Scotland remained a royal residence, which was particularly appreciated by Queen Victoria. She spent much time at Holyroodhouse, despite the fact that thoughts of its gloomy past plunged her into melancholy. On every visit she was compulsively drawn to the room "where the unfortunate Mary Stuart was dining when poor Rizzio was murdered."

1

3

THE BODY OF
DAVID RIZZIO
WAS INTERRED AFTER HIS MURDER
IN QUEEN MARY'S SUPPER ROOM
9TH MARCH. 1566.

4

5

# A Tudor Jewel
# HAMPTON COURT near London

**HAMPTON COURT PALACE**
England, near London,
1514–1737
Commissioned by: Cardinal
Thomas Wolsey
Architects: Sir Christopher
Wren, from 1689, et al.

Thomas Wolsey basked in his glory. In rapid succession he had advanced from Archbishop of York to Cardinal and Lord Chancellor, the most important advisor to King Henry VIII of England (1509–47). Personally thrifty but by dint of his office a lover of luxury, and thus virtually schizophrenic, the second man in the state wished to reside in a manner in keeping with his position. So, twenty-five kilometers southwest of London, in a bend of the Thames, Wolsey had a palace of superlatives erected.

From the beginning, fairy-tale luxury reigned at Hampton Court, once the largest palatial complex in Europe. Its exquisite textiles and gobelins, its chairs, tables, chests, and beds were among the costliest that were to be had. Wolsey ordered the curtains, interwoven with gold, from Venice, and the pearl-embroidered cushions from the Near East. When Henry VIII first saw Hampton Court, it roused his envy. The magnificence of his "good cardinal" was beyond his means. There was only one remedy—to strip Wolsey of power and confiscate all his possessions. An excuse soon presented itself. Henry VIII, though a married man, had fallen hopelessly in love with

*The Grand Hall of Hampton Court still stems from the days of King Henry VIII. The mighty edifice, into which we entered as if into the central aisle of a Gothic church, saw the sunrise of Anne Boleyn. And even now, our eye still discerns the insignia A and H (Anne and Henry) like a picture of their one- ness—letters perhaps being incised as the blade of the axe already hovered over the lovely lady's neck.*

Theodore Fontane, *A Picnic at Hampton Court*, 1854

a young noblewoman by the name of Anne Boleyn, and wished to legitimize the relationship. To do so a papal annulment of his marriage with Catherine of Aragon was required.

The cardinal did his best, but the negotiations with Rome failed. Wolsey fell out of favor with the king, lost all his offices, and was accused of high treason. Only a stroke of fate saved him from the gallows—on the journey to London for trial, the cardinal died of dysentery.

By this time Henry VIII was already holding his first uproarious festivities at Hampton Court, at his side Anne Boleyn, whom he would finally wed with the blessing of the Anglican Church he had founded for this very purpose. Surrounded by no less than five hundred servants, the couple spent their honeymoon at their new favorite home, and planned to expand it at incredible expense. First came a beer cellar, bowling alleys, and a covered tennis court, because "tennys," played with felt balls stuffed with dog's hair, was the king's great passion. In

addition, Hampton Court received one of the most modern, water-flushed toilets of the day, which permitted twenty-eight people at a time to answer the call of nature. The most magnificent room and heart of the palace is the Great Hall, under whose soaring beamed ceiling dazzling receptions and banquets were held.

Yet Anne Boleyn's days at Hampton Court were numbered. Her husband had long become interested in another young lady. To pave the way for her, Henry VIII had Anne Boleyn charged with adultery, and on May 19, 1536, she was beheaded in the Tower of London. Not twenty-four hours later Henry wedded Jane Seymour at Hampton Court, as his retinue maintained an icy silence. But Jane would die in childbed only a year later. Ever since, legend has it, Hampton Court has been haunted by her ghost, wandering by night through the chambers of the clock tower with a long flickering candle.

1 Leonard Knyff, *Panoramic View of the Palace in George I's Time*, 1714–27
2 Portrait of Cardinal Thomas Wolsey
3 View of the entrance front of the Tudor palace
4 One of Henry VIII's love letters to Anne Boleyn
5 The garden facade, designed by Sir Christopher Wren, 1689–92

3

4

5

# CHÂTEAU OF CHAMBORD Loire Valley

The peasants of the Loire Valley avoided the ruined castle, for on certain autumn nights, they said, the sounds of a ghostly hunting party were to be heard, although no one was to be seen. Francis I of France, a passionate hunter, was not put off by such tall tales. The region was famous for its abundant game, and the abandoned spot in the midst of great tracts of forest seemed perfect for a palace that, Francis declared, would outshine anything ever built before. In 1519, he hired 1,800 day laborers to demolish the ruins of the old castle, ram hundreds of oak trunks into the swampy ground, lay a limestone founda-

*One might well think that an oriental djinn had spirited the Château de Chambord somewhere out of the Orient. For in view of its cupolas, towerlets, and miniature spires one would presume it stood in the Kingdom of Bagdad or Kashmir—if the mossy walls and gloomy sky did not clearly attest to the fact that one finds oneself in a land of rain.*

Alfred de Vigny, *Cinq-Mars: or, A Conspiracy under Louis XIII*, 1826

CHÂTEAU OF CHAMBORD
France, Loire Valley, 1519–59

tion, and erect a palace in the form of a Greek cross—the largest, most modern, and original of all the castles on the Loire.

Even Emperor Charles V was impressed. In 1539 the ruler of the Holy Roman Empire dwelled in an apartment lined with damask, velvet, and taffeta, and praised the château as the "quintessence of that, which human art is capable of creating." Victor Hugo, too, was taken by the palace's unprecedented beauty, noting "United in the

admirable eccentricity of this fairy-tale and chivalric palace is all magic, all poetry, indeed all madness." Many a dazzled viewer truly thought Chambord the work of a sorcerer—not least on account of the massive double-spiral stair tower in the center of the three-story main building. This likely went back to a drawing by Leonardo da Vinci, for its twofold turn recalled early turbine designs by the universal genius and was considered an engineering wonder.

Francis I followed the progress of building with great interest. Yet he never actually lived in Chambord for any length of time, since back then it had neither a kitchen nor furniture. Every time he went there to hunt, he brought quantities of furnishings along: wardrobes, bunk beds, tapestries, and gobelins that temporarily lent the bare rooms a certain comfort. Female companionship helped as well. At times, Francis reputedly gathered no less than twenty-seven ladies around him, declaring that "a court without ladies is like a year without spring and a spring without roses." That his life was nevertheless not always a rose garden, may be gathered from a sentence Francis scratched into a window of his apartment: "Women are capricious. Unfortunate the man who trusts them."

Still, no greater hardships than this were to befall the king. The ghostly shades he had been warned of never appeared. When in the wake of the French Revolution the palace was to be razed as a symbol of the monarchy, it was saved by an art-loving official who made such a high estimate of demolition costs, that the shocked iconoclasts abandoned their plans.

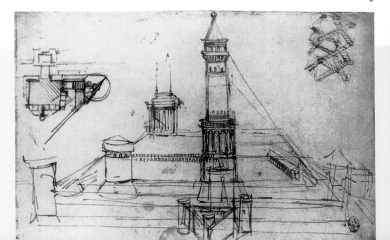

1 Detail of the rooftops
2 Sketch for a staircase, fortifications, and a lantern, pen-and-ink drawing by Leonardo da Vinci, between 1516 and 1519
3 Francis I at the meet, wall hanging after Larent Guyot, early seventeenth century
4 Like a mirage: the Château of Chambord
5 The double-spiral stair tower inside the château
6 Aerial view of the overall complex

6

5

# NOORDEINDE PALACE   The Hague

NOORDEINDE PALACE
The Netherlands, The Hague,
1530–1984
Architects: Willem Goudt,
Jacob van Campen, Pieter
Post, et al.

Queen Sophie of The Netherlands (1818–77) was elated. The coronation of her husband, William III, had finally made it possible to move out of the dark and musty crown prince's palace. Now the young couple occupied Noordeinde—an elegant, bright and airy little palace at the "north end" of the old city of The Hague. Sophie described the effect of the change of scene to a friend as being as "happy as a child." The queen blossomed—and temporarily forgot she did not even like The Netherlands. How Sophie, born Princess of Württemberg, had yearned for the rolling hills of her southern German home on dreary gray days in the flatlands, and how debilitating the prudish way of life of the Dutch nobility had seemed to her.

*In the meantime I have moved with William into the freshly renovated Noordeinde Palais. However, the artisans are still at work in my private apartments, so that at the moment comfort leaves much to be desired. I am nevertheless happy to be here—the marvelous garden, the pretty salon, and the light-flooded rooms are wonderful amenities, which I have missed terribly these past years. These things do mean so much to a woman.*

Queen Sophie of The Netherlands, in a letter of May 18, 1849, to her friend Lady Malet

After the move, all this no longer mattered. While her husband occupied a large apartment on the ground floor of the palace, Sophie lived on the floor above with her sons, surrounded by servants and nannies. The windows opened on the garden, and the furnishings were of the finest to be had. The curtains were of white satin, the furniture of mahogany, the oil lamps of hand-painted porcelain. The queen conducted her extensive correspondence with heads of state and international intellectuals from a desk whose writing surface was adorned by intarsia work of rose and lemon wood. When she felt like musical diversion, she could sit down at a grand piano from a renowned Parisian firm. The only thing lacking was a ballroom.

This was rapidly ordered, but construction ran into delays. It was finally inaugurated on March 14, 1862—with an exhilarating masquerade ball illuminated by thousands of candles. "His costume from the period of Louis XIII suited the king superbly," wrote Sophie a few days afterwards in a letter, "but the greatest attention was attracted by our eldest son, the crown prince. He appeared in Greek garb and had a charming girl at his side. Actually he is not at all vain. Yet with his fine features he stood out so stunningly from the great mass of the otherwise so ugly young men that he would have every reason to be conceited."

The brilliant festivities at which Sophie and William III played the perfect hosts became legendary. Yet behind the scenes, the highly educated, intellectually superior queen joked about her ineffectual husband, about whom even well-wishing biographers said that "his impulsive manner, his rather haphazard way of thinking, and his aversion to persistent effort in conducting state business proved an obstacle to an optimum use of his royal position." William III avenged himself for the ignominy by excluding the queen from all government activities and consoling himself with extramarital escapades. For Sophie, life became a torment.

Even her beloved palace lost its luster. Increasingly isolated from the king's affairs and condemned to idleness, she spent her days alone in her chambers. And when their second-oldest son died of a mysterious illness at Noordeinde, Sophie fell into a profound depression. "Life at this palace is terrible," she confessed to a friend. "You could cut the air in the rooms with a knife—and a horribly unhealthy odor lies over everything." Completely embittered, the "queen of queens," as she was admiringly known to her contemporaries, died on June 3, 1877.

1

2

1  After the masquerade ball on March 14, 1862.
   *Le Souper*, watercolor by C. ten Kate
2  Noordeinde Palace became the official seat of the
   Dutch royal family in 1984
3  King William III and Queen Sophie at the masquerade ball
   wearing costumes from the time of Louis XIII. *Le Buffet*,
   painting by C. ten Kate
4  The large anteroom

3

4

# FONTAINEBLEAU PALACE Fontainebleau

FONTAINEBLEAU PALACE
France, Fontainebleau,
1528–1782
Architects: Gilles Le Breton,
Pierre Chambiges the Elder,
Philibert Delorme, Jacques-
Ange Gabriel, et al.

When Napoleon Bonaparte (1769–1821) saw Fontainebleau Palace for the first time, in 1801, he merely shook his head. The suites were empty and plundered, the wood paneling crumbling with rot, the murals covered with mildew. There was not a single door left in the palace, let alone a windowpane. During the days of the Revolution, everything that had not been nailed down had been taken by the locals. In substance, however, the building was still intact, and was worth putting back in order.

No sooner had first repairs been made than the venerable walls began to reverberate with fresh life. In the wing now bordering today's English Garden on the north, a cadet academy opened its doors. Yet this would not be all. Napoleon grew increasingly fond of the palace sixty kilometers southeast of Paris, which for centuries had been a favorite refuge of French monarchs.

The forested idyll with its virtually inexhaustible hunting grounds had been discovered around 1200, by Louis

*Napoleon appeared on the landing of the grand stairway at Fontainebleau Palace, gazed down into the Cour de'honneur where his troops had formed ranks, and raised his voice: "Men, I bid you farewell. I am going. Do not mourn my fate. I would like to press all of you to my heart. So at least let me embrace your general and your flag!" The entire army broke out in tears and a long, low sigh was their only answer.*

Alphonse de Lamartine, *History of the Restoration*, 1815

1 View of the palace complex
2 The *Grand Galerie*
3 Napoleon bidding farewell to his troops, by Jean-Pierre-Marie Jazet after Horace Vernet, 1825
4 View through the palace gates on to the Cour du Cheval Blanc
5 Legend has it that carp from the Napoleonic era still swim in the palace pond

the Fat. Louis the Saint called Fontainebleau "my beloved wilderness." Philip the Bold believed that its pure air was proof against the plague, which is why Philip the Fair, his son, first saw the light of the world in Fontainebleau, where he would also leave the world forty-six years later. Francis I had the oldest tracts of the present-day palace built on the site of the former pleasure seat. The complex as it now stands includes annexes added by Henry II, Henry IV, and Louis XV.

2

Napoleon was keen to join this illustrious circle of royal contractors and inhabitants, intending to outshine their glory with his imperial majesty. To this end the Corsican was willing to endure certain hardships. During his first stays at Fontainebleau the walls had only makeshift coverings, furniture was scarce, and it was terribly drafty. Yet gradually Napoleon transformed the palace into a comfortable residence. He spent a fortune on restoration. When it was finished, Fontainebleau Palace shone more gloriously than ever. Most of the apartments had been entirely refurnished and redecorated, and Napoleon's emblem—a great golden "N" encompassed by a laurel wreath—adorned fireplaces and doors, tables and chairs. The former royal bedroom was now the imperial throne room. "The new marshals, the new princes paraded at festivities, which were resplendent with youth, glory, and new uniforms. Thousands of people inhabited the palace," one biographer described that time.

Yet the Napoleonic era in Fontainebleau was short-lived. Declared deposed, the emperor signed his abdication papers on April 6, 1814, in the Red Salon of the *Grands Appartements*. A fortnight later, just before leaving the country, he said farewell to his troops in moving words. The site of this memorable occasion, the Cour d'honneur of Fontainebleau, has been known as *Cour des Adieux* ever since.

1

3

# GRIPSHOLM CASTLE near Mariefried

GRIPSHOLM CASTLE
Sweden, near Mariefried,
1553–1783
Architects: Heinrich von
Cöllen, Nicodemus Tessin the
Younger, et al.

He loved pseudonyms. As "Ignaz Wrobel" he wrote acid political commentaries, as "Peter Panter" witty feuilletons, and melancholy observations as "Kaspar Hauser." When he felt a bit roguish, he would sign his letters "Martha Knautschke, landlady, who has seen better days." In reality the man's name was Kurt Tucholsky (1890–1935). A native of Berlin, he was a doctor of law, earned his living by writing, and yearned, from early childhood, for the Far North: "It begins in Middle Germany, where the air stands so clear over the roofs, and the farther northwards one goes, the louder one's heart begins to beat."

It beat loudest in Sweden, where Tucholsky went looking for a place to stay in the spring of 1929. Fifty kilometers west of Stockholm he found what he was looking for: "Mariefried is a tiny little town on Lake Mälar. Nature there was still and peaceful, trees and meadows, fields and woods—but no one would have taken notice of this place were it not the site of one of the oldest castles in Sweden: Gripsholm."

As early as 1383 the island just off the coast contained a fortified castle, on whose ruins King Gustavus 1 Adolphus had the core building of the present-day complex

a sort of pantheon. King Charles ix had portraits of honorable citizens hung throughout the castle, thus laying the cornerstone of one of Europe's largest portrait collections, continually supplemented down to the present day. "Many lovely paintings hung there," Tucholsky recalled. But "they meant nothing to me."

However, the atmosphere of the castle did inspire him, to write what he called a "summer story." It appeared in 1931, and found an enthusiastic echo in the international press. The story's title: *Gripsholm Castle.* Admittedly, in the novel the island residence serves as little more than an enchanting backdrop: "The castle slept heavy and still," we read, "everywhere it smelled of water and wood that had long lay in the sun, of fish and ducks." Although this description may have jibed with Tucholsky's impression, the rest is pure fiction. Unlike his protagonists, the author never stayed in the castle with its old furniture in a "heavy, comfortable style." Nor does his statement that Gripsholm had a dungeon "in which Gustavus the Constipated had kept the Unshaven imprisoned for years" accord with the historical facts, at least as far as the figures' names are concerned.

Yet one thing seems truly to have moved the author to the bottom of his heart: "There stands Gripsholm. Why don't we just stay here forever?" his hero wonders. "One might, for instance, take a long-term lease here, make a contract with the lady of the castle, which would certainly not be very expensive, and then for all time to come: blue air, gray air, sun, sea's breath, fish, and grog—eternal, eternal holiday." As if wishing to make these lines come true, at least figuratively, Tucholsky expressed the desire to be buried at the cemetery in Mariefried. Indeed, he was buried there in view of the castle in 1935.

> *It was a very bright day. The castle, built of red brick, stood there radiant, its round cupolas shot into the sky— this edifice was heavy, a stolid fort. I know nothing about the style of this castle—all I know is that if I were ever to build myself one, I would build one like this.*
>
> Kurt Tucholsky, *Gripsholm Castle*, 1931

erected. The massive cannon towers with their meters-thick walls, secret corridors, and spiral staircases, date from the sixteenth century. The cupolas were not added until 1730–50, when the erstwhile fort was gradually converted into a comfortable castle. Up to that point Gripsholm had served almost exclusively as a home for the widows of Swedish kings. Now the historical building developed into a scene of glorious receptions—and into

1 The writer Kurt Tucholsky emigrated in 1929 from Germany to Sweden and spent some time living near the castle
2 The idyllic castle on Lake Mälar
3 Gustavus III started using Gripsholm Castle as his residence in 1773

2

3

# The Throne of Spain
# ALCÁZAR Toledo

Although "the most Spanish of all Spanish cities" does not lie on the sea, the fish market was well stocked, even in the sixteenth century. From wooden crates full of ice, vendors offered every conceivable culinary delicacy from the ocean's depths. Emperor Charles v (1500–58) break-

*The colossal block of rock, embraced on three sides by the Tagus River, is marvellous to behold. It is like a jewelry setting with a brilliant gem in the center. This precious stone is imperial Toledo itself. Above the roofs of the imperial city thrones the manorial Alcázar. It makes the evil shiver, but leaves the good untroubled.*

Maurice Barrès, *Greco, or The Mystery of Toledo*, 1911

fasted on eel pâté, fresh oysters, sardines, and anchovies, washed down with a nicely chilled beer. Apart from such treats of the table, he was intrigued by the city's past. Toledo—at 50,000 inhabitants the most populous metropolis in Castile at the time—was among the oldest and culturally richest cities in Spain.

Its imposing location had already been appreciated by the Romans. Later, the Western Goths ruled their empire from here. But it was the Moorish period in which Toledo experienced its heyday. From the eighth to the eleventh century the city was a melting pot of cultures, a mecca of Christian, Jewish, and Islamic scholarship, the "Castilian Jerusalem." The fame of those days was still reverberating, and the mild climate and picturesque lanes did the rest when, in late April 1525, Charles v fell in love with the city on his first visit. He declared it "queen of the empire," lent it his imperial coat of arms, and had the Alcázar converted into a residence.

It would become the most magnificent of its kind in the Western world. The old, drafty castle, with its diverse tracts from different eras was demolished, except for a few walls and vaulted ceilings, to make way for a nearly square palace, which today rises like a monolith above the tumult of the city's roofs.

The apartments where Charles v received such men as Hernán Cortéz and Francisco Pizarro, conquerors of Mexico and Peru, were so luxuriously furnished that a well-traveled contemporary declared he had seen nothing

ALCÁZAR
Spain, Toledo, 1537–78
Architects: Alonso de Covarrubias, Francisco Villalpando, Hernan Gonzáles de Lara, Gaspar de la Vega, Juan de Herrera, et al.

to compare with them. Charles v used to say that he did not really feel like a true emperor until he entered the Alcázar in Toledo. This, however, was not often vouchsafed him. As "lord of the world," who had himself titled in documents as "Roman Emperor, King of Germany, Castile, Aragón, Léon, the Baleares, the Canary and Indian Islands, both Sicilies, Jerusalem, Hungary, Dalmatia, Croatia, Navarra, Mexico, Peru, etc., etc.," Charles v lived what amounted to a nomadic life. All in all, he likely spent little more than a few months in Toledo.

Still, one confronts him everywhere in his former residential city even today. A monument to him stands in the arcade court of the Alcázar, and his coat of arms graces the Puerta Nueva de Bisagra, the northern city gate. There is also a lane named after him. This was once the home of Juanello Torriano, a talented mechanic. For the emperor, who was obsessed with such things, Torriano constructed clocks and other automatic apparatus, supposedly including a life-size articulated doll that could walk and bore an astonishing resemblance to Charles v. Legend has it that even years after the emperor's death, this doll would unexpectedly appear at one street corner or another, convincing the Toledans, if only for a brief moment, that Charles v was indeed still alive. *The Calle del hombre de palo*, or "Lane of the Wooden Man," is named after it.

1

3

1  Toledo remained the spiritual center of Spain, even after Philip II
   proclaimed Madrid the capital in 1561
2  *Charles V and his Consort, Isabella of Portugal,* painting by
   Peter-Paul Rubens, after Titian, 1628–29
3  *View of Toledo,* painting by El Greco, c. 1597

2

He had begun to wonder whether his childless uncle, Frederick II, would ever die. But then his ancient relative finally passed away, and Otto Henry (1502–59) could at last, as Elector of the Palatinate, take possession of Heidelberg Castle Hill. At fifty-four, he himself was no longer young and suffered from various aches and pains. His "bodily dilapidation," as he called it, was not surprising, seeing that he now weighed close to four hundred pounds. Climbing stairs was a thing of the past for him, so when he wished to attend church services down in the town, he had to squeeze himself into a sedan chair and be carried on mule-back.

*Nowhere does the sun set in such glory and radiant color as in Heidelberg. The castle ruins stand in such a magical rosy light and the banks of the Neckar are bordered in such a bright gold that a faithful painting of them would be put down as exaggerated.*

From a travel guide, *Heidelberg, Mannheim and Schwetzingen for Travelers*, 1808

Yet, Otto Henry loved not only opulent dining and fine vintages; his enthusiasms ranged from foreign lands and peoples to exotic animals, alchemistic experiments, medical treatises, and learned debates, especially about art: he owned bronzes from Florence, tapestries from Brussels, paintings by Cranach, Dürer, and Titian. Such an aesthete was he, that he had the tails of the horses at his court dyed red and blue. And, as he himself admitted, Otto Henry had been bitten by the "building bug." From France, Italy, and The Netherlands he ordered the latest books on architecture, and plans, and views of famous sights. Then he set to work.

HEIDELBERG CASTLE
Otto Henry Building,
Germany, Heidelberg,
1556–59
Architect: Heinrich Gut (?),
Facade ornament: Alexander
Colin

While his predecessors had built drafty lodgings, Otto Henry erected a palace. The Otto Henry Building (Ottheinrichsbau) was once the most outstanding architectural feature of the Heidelberg Castle complex. Its richly ornamented, sculpture-adorned facade was a superb example of aristocratic self-representation,

uniquely reflecting the interests of its builder. Figures of Planet Gods stood for Otto Henry's involvement with astrology, and the Virtues symbolized his ideals as a ruler. Busts of Roman emperors were inspired by his coin collection, and instruments represented his love of music. A Hercules figure embodied Otto Henry as the herald of a new era.

The achievements of his reign were truly remarkable. He introduced Lutheranism and empirical science, founded one of the most significant libraries in Europe, the Bibliotheca Palatina, and made Heidelberg into a glorious center of German humanism. Today his palace is nothing but a ruin. Yet his myth lives on, thanks not least to a surviving piece of Otto Henry's clothing—a knitted jacket measuring over two-and-one-half meters around the chest.

1 *Hortus Palatinus*, oil painting by Jacques Fouquières, 1620
2 Detail of the Otto Henry Building's ornate facade
3 Knitted jacket belonging to Otto Henry, Elector of the Palatinate, c. 1550
4 Inner courtyard of the castle, left is the Frederick Building, and on the right is the Otto Henry Building
5 View over the Neckar River, the city, and Heidelberg Castle

# EL ESCORIAL near Madrid

The king dreamed of seclusion. That is why Philip II (1556–98), the most devoutly Catholic of all then-reigning monarchs, desired a new residence outside Madrid, but not too far outside. He envisioned a Castle of God—a "monument to the True Faith" where he could immerse himself ever more deeply in the devout practices that were so important to him. Fifty kilometers northwest of Madrid, at the foot of the Sierra de Guadarrama, the commission formed to search for a suitable site found one—a village the inhabitants called "El Escorial," the "Slag Heap," above which rose a mighty rock plateau.

This place, where ore had once been mined and smelted, seemed perfectly suited to the god-fearing monarch's vision. On April 23, 1563, Philip II laid the cornerstone of El Escorial. Over the following two decades an army of laborers transformed the plateau,

> *As rapidly as possible a palace and monastery were to be built, a fortress that would serve simultaneously as a bastion of the Most Holy and a tomb for the king. No pomp and no magnificence. No divagation from the inexorably rigorous plan conceived by the king. The sole ornament of the palace, which appears wrested from the mountains like the surrounding rocks, would be the Cross, the symbol of Christianity.*
>
> Carlos Fuentes, in *Terra Nostra*, 1975

1,100 meters above sea level, into the biggest construction site in the Western world. It was said that Philip observed the progress of work with a telescope, from a window of his Madrid palace. He regularly stayed at the parsonage in the neighboring village to see how things were progressing. He was reputedly also on hand when the enormous granite blocks for the main portal were delivered—on wagons drawn by as many as forty oxen.

The royal family spent their first night at the labyrinthine complex on June 11–12, 1571. Nothing was finished except for the private apartments, which even today recall monastic cells more than princely chambers. Philip II's study contains only an armchair, a simple wooden table, and a plain bookcase. The bedroom is similarly bare, its only decorations being a crucifix and a painting by Hieronymus Bosch, *The Seven Deadly Sins*. The expansive palace, served simultaneously as a monastery, royal sepulcher, library, and garrison, and was not intended as a temple of *joie de vivre*—although there were carefree days at the Escorial, even in Philip II's times.

The entire court once reportedly gathered one evening when an elephant trainer arrived with his colorfully decked out animals. There was also celebrating when the villagers came to dance under the palace windows, where they were rewarded with leg of mutton, liver-omelets, and quince jam. Yet the king, invariably clad in black, kept aloof from such goings-on, preferring to peruse stacks of documents or kneel at the feet of saintly images and relics in order to make decisions that would find approval in the eyes of God. Toward the end, only his daughters, to whom he wrote tender letters and whom he even advised in fashion matters, remained faithful to their eccentric father. Everyone else at court crossed themselves three times in relief when their feared master died at Escorial shortly before sunrise on September 13, 1598, and became one of the first to be buried in the crypt of his palace church.

EL ESCORIAL
Spain, near Madrid, 1563–84
Architects: Juan Bautista
de Toledo and Juan de
Herrera

2

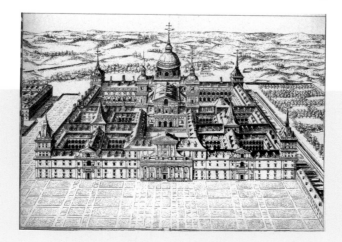

1  Portrait of *King Philip II*, painting by Coello Alonso Sanchez, c. 1568
2  The ground plan was laid out as a huge rectangle measuring 210 x 170 meters, seen here in an etching by Abraham Ortelius
3  View from the Sierra de Guadarrama
4  The library
5  The Escorial crypt, burial site of countless Spanish kings

3

4    5

# ARANJUEZ PALACE Aranjuez

"Aranjuez is a gift of the River Tagus," wrote an early Spanish historian. He was right, because thanks to the humid river valley in which it runs, a blossoming, wooded oasis lies here in the midst of the bare Castilian *meseta*. Spanish rulers discovered this idyllic spot fifty kilometers south of Madrid as early as the fifteenth century, and used to frequent it especially in the spring.

*I see the water as it flows transparent and fast over a low weir near the palace; I see the swans with their faces, as if made-up, above snowy feathers; I see the reddish walls of the palace, that already stood when Schiller wrote that line which still draws people there even today: "Alas," said the monk Domingo to the unfortunate, ill-fated Don Carlos, "the lovely days at Aranjuez have come to an end."*

Cees Noteboom, *The Lovely Days at Aranjuez*, 2001

1

Nowhere else, it was said, did awakening nature present her perfumes and colors in more variety and charm than at Aranjuez.

King Philip II, at whose behest the core building of today's palace with its facade of white limestone and red "brick kilned in the Flemish manner," loved Aranjuez especially. He had the expansive park laid out, ordered shady elms from England, as well as trees, roses, and jasmine from France. Still, the stringent monarch's sojourns were not to be all too pleasurable. When he coasted in his opulent bark along the still waters of the canals, "he took a desk along on which he worked out contracts or studied files, as musicians on the banks played the guitar and ladies of the court danced," as one biographer reported. In the eighteenth century the park, to which Joaquin Rodrigo set a musical monument with his *Concierto de Aranjuez*, even entered world literature, when Friedrich Schiller envisioned the first act of his drama *Don Carlos*, playing "in the royal garden of Aranjuez." Admittedly, the great German author idealized his hero. The talented, magnanimous heir to the throne, who, in contrast to his father, King Philip II, advocated enlightened thought and a modern idea of the state, was largely an invention.

At any rate, contemporaries had little good to say about the historical Don Carlos (1545–68), who often stayed at Aranjuez Palace with his family. As the Venetian emissary Federico Badoero noted in 1557, the twelve-year-old Infante was "proud, impetuous, and of a cruel nature." He was said to have "had rabbits roasted alive" and bitten off the head of a turtle that had snapped at his finger. Nor did Don Carlos make an any more convincing impression in later years: "He is very immature for his age, unpredictable, loves no one, hates many, and tends more to hurt than to benefit," one observer described the twenty-one-year-old.

Nobody thought him capable of ruling the Spanish empire. Finally he was arrested on order of his own father. The reasons for this are still a source of speculation. Had Don Carlos become dangerous? Was he planning to murder his father? Or intending to escape from the oppressive atmosphere of the court? Or had he fallen in love at Aranjuez with his stepmother, who had originally been promised him as a wife? Philip II maintained his silence on such questions, and Don Carlos could no longer answer them. After six months' imprisonment he died in the morning hours of July 24, 1568, of unexplained causes. For the twenty-three-year-old heir, as Schiller wrote, "the lovely days at Aranjuez" had come to an end—if there had in fact been any at all in the first place.

ARANJUEZ PALACE
Spain, Aranjuez, 1564–1778
Architects: Juan Bautista de Toledo, Jerónimo Gili, Juan de Herrera, Juan Gómez de Mora, Giacomo Bonavía, Francisco Sabatini, et al.

1

2

1  View of the palace's main
   facade
2  *Hunting at Aranjuez*, painting
   by Luan Bautista Martínez del
   Mazo, 17th century
3  *Veduta* of Aranjuez Palace
4  Philip II and his family,
   bronze figures at El Escorial
   by Pompeo Leoni, 1598. The
   group comprises King Philip II
   and his second wife in the
   front row and his first wife
   with their son, Don Carlos,
   and his spouse, Elizabeth of
   Valois, in the second row

IMPERIAL PALACE
Japan, Tokyo, 1603–1970

Japanese officials proved extremely choosy with regard to the gifts that guests were allowed to give to the emperor. When they heard that Dutch merchants invited to an audience intended to present him with a rare bird, a superb example of its species, the officials politely declined. According to the description submitted, the bird was so large that they feared it would eat too much. Even a brand-new brass fire engine, which Europeans thought a perfect gift in view of the frequent fires that ravaged Japan's mostly wooden palaces, found no approval, as recorded in the diaries of Engelbert Kaempfer (1651–1716).

Kaempfer, a widely traveled pastor's son, medical man, and natural scientist from northern Germany, lived in Japan from 1690–92 as a doctor in the employ of the

*Among the imperial trade cities, Edo is the principal one: the residence of the emperor and, due to the great holdings of court and the presence of all the noble families of the land, the largest and most distinguished in the whole empire. The bay along whose shores it spreads gives the city the form of a half moon.*

Engelbert Kaempfer, *The History of Japan: Together with a Description of the Kingdom of Siam 1690–1692*

Dutch East India Trading Company. He was privy to a privilege that was just about unparalleled at the time. On March 29, 1692, Kaempfer and a delegation of Dutch merchants were received by the Japanese emperor in Edo, today's Tokyo. The busy metropolis—boasting some one million inhabitants, making it one of the largest cities in the world even then—was not to become the capital of the country until 1868. Yet from as early as 1603,

Edo was considered the political center of Japan. It was the seat of the shogun, supreme commander of the armed forces and the true ruler of the country.

The emperors, divested of secular power, stood in the shoguns' shadow until far into the nineteenth century, reduced to the function of spiritual head of state with few official duties. Still, the people revered the emperor as the Tennô, the Most Exalted or Son of Heaven. Only very high-ranking princes and courtiers were permitted to meet him in person; commoners and foreigners not at all. Each audience was governed by strict ritual. Kaempfer, after describing the opulent interior of the Imperial Palace with its richly gilded carvings, exquisite inlay work, and walls painted in many colors, continues, "After we had waited for over an hour, the officials called our captain into the audience hall. There he had to drop to his knees and, crawl on all fours to the raised throne of His Imperial Majesty. There he had to bow his head to the floor as he thanked the emperor for the goodwill which had enabled our company to conduct free trade in Japan. Then he in turn retreated on all fours, like a crab scuttling backwards, to his point of departure."

But this was not all. After the audience, the delegation was escorted "deeper into the palace," in order to be introduced to the empress, the princesses, and other ladies "for their pleasure and scrutiny." Even the emperor joined the party, if concealed behind a screen, and requested his guests "to take off our cloaks and festive dress and perform all sorts of pranks, walk back and forth, then dance, imitate a drunken man, stammer Japanese, paint, read in Dutch and German—and sing." The relief of the Dutchmen was great when the emperor declared the audience ended. "But the officials congratulated us. Because never before had foreign merchants experienced such an extraordinarily honorable reception at the imperial court of Edo."

1  The Imperial Palace, c. 1900
2  The palace is approached via the "Double Bridge" (Niju-bashi), so called because of its reflection in the water
3  An aerial view of the palace complex

1

2

3

# HELLBRUNN PALACE   Salzburg

1

This clergyman was no child of melancholy, quite the contrary. When Markus Sittikus von Hohenems became Prince Bishop of Salzburg at age thirty-eight, his first concern was to plan the upcoming Carnival. He immediately thought up all sorts of diversions, especially of a kind designed to heighten the merrymaking. Not only did he encourage his servants, the kitchen staff, and even members of the court building department to don masks and parade through the lanes of the town, but headed the colorful procession himself, in fancy costume.

No wonder people thought the jolly bishop capable of most anything. Soon Markus Sittikus was rumored to be having a passionate affair with Ursula von Mabon, wife of his captain of guards. Perhaps this explains why his sermons seem so natural, heartfelt, and full of *joie de vivre*.

> *Oh what a lovely retreat, what a charming refuge of delight, what an earthly paradise. It proves itself more than worthy of its light-flooded name, Hellbrunn [literally, "bright fountain"]. For its waters are clearer than glass, purer than crystal, and even more transparent than the radiance of the sky. Hellbrunn is a maze of cool springs, a gamboling of naiads, a theater of flowers, a museum of the Graces.*
>
> Domenico Ghisberti, *The Journey of the Elector of Bavaria to Salzburg*, 1670

Whatever the case, nothing human was apparently foreign to him. This prince of the church loved luxury. An aficionado of everything Italian, Markus Sittikus built himself a pleasure seat outside the town gates in the style of a Roman villa—the earliest example of its kind north of the Alps.

**HELLBRUNN PALACE**
Austria, Salzburg, 1613–19
Architect: Santino Solari

Envisaged from the start as a place of amusement, Hellbrunn was chock full of curiosities and surprises, a *theatrum mundi* of exotic plants, rare animals, artificial ruins, and enchanted grottoes. Plus a few practical jokes for good measure. To hold festive summer dinners, Markus Sittikus had a "princely table" with ten stone stools set up outdoors. One of these, reserved for his own use, remained unaltered. Guests were invited to take their seats on the other nine stools, and if the carousing threatened to get out of hand, the bishop could trigger jets of water from nozzles concealed in the seats.

Indeed, water played a leading role at Hellbrunn Palace park, which is rich in natural springs. Apart from hidden nozzles, fountains, ponds, and ingenious water follies, the park still contains the five oldest, still functioning, water-powered automatons in Europe. One, known as the *Germaul*, thirty centimeters in height and made of painted copper, is a caricature of a man's face with huge ears, equipped with a hydraulic mechanism that causes the eyes to roll and the tongue to protrude. It reputedly represents Markus Sittikus himself, and implies that he thought absolutely nothing of criticisms of his quite unclerical way of life.

1 Portrait of the Prince Archbishop Markus Sittikus with Hellbrunn Palace in the background. Oil painting attributed to Donato Mascagni, 1618. In his hand a picture of the uncompleted Salzburg Cathedral, the construction of which was likewise commissioned by him
2 The garden front of the palace
3 Roman theater with hydraulic waterworks and the "princely table"
4 Mechanical theater in which life in a small Baroque town is shown

2

3          4

# POTALA PALACE  Lhasa

**POTALA PALACE**
Tibet, Lhasa, 1645–94

With their matted beards and tattered clothes, the two men looked more like highway robbers than civilized travelers. But the Austrian alpinist Heinrich Harrer, born in 1912, and his friend Peter Aufschnaiter had been through arduous months, having crossed sixty-five high mountain passes to reach their goal. Finally, they stood at the western gate of the sacred city of Lhasa—the "mysterious citadel, illuminated by the magic of centuries, of the great Dalai Lama," as an old travel report had described it. The sight was overwhelming: Potala Palace, the winter seat of the spiritual head of the Tibetans, rose mightily into a steel-blue sky.

Perched on the Red Cliff, the compelling landmark of Lhasa, the structure consists of thirteen stories, each rising stepwise above the next. Legend has it that the palace was a work of the good spirits. Its contractor was purportedly the 5th Dalai Lama, whose death in 1682 was kept secret for twelve years, because when he died it was feared that the conscripted laborers, as soon as they heard their master was no longer among them, would flee the building site leaving the palace unfinished.

Harrer and Aufschnaiter soon met the barely thirteen-year-old Dalai Lama. The Tibetan ruler, believed to be the fourteenth incarnation of the Buddha, invited the two

*It was January 15th, 1946, when we set out on our last march. From Tölung we came into the broad valley of Kyichu. We turned a corner and saw, gleaming in the distance, the golden roofs of Potala, the winter residence of the Dalai Lama and the most famous landmark of Lhasa. This moment compensated us for much. We felt inclined to go down on our knees like the pilgrims and touch the ground with our foreheads... Now all that was forgotten as we gazed at the golden pinnacles—six miles more and we had reached our goal.*

Heinrich Harrer, *Seven Years in Tibet*, 1952

strangers, who were already the talk of the town, to an audience–thus fulfilling a wish they would never dared to have uttered: permission to enter the most holy sanctuary of Tibet. "Dark corridors, their walls decorated with paintings of strange protecting deities, led through the ground-floor buildings to a courtyard. From there steep ladders, several floors high, took one up to the flat roof. The visitors solemnly ascended them. Up above, a dense crowd was already assembled, as everyone has the right to receive the Great One's blessing at the New Year. On the roof there were a number of small buildings with gilded roofs. These were the apartments of the Dalai Lama. In the posture of the Buddha, leaning slightly

forward, the Dalai Lama was sitting on a throne covered with costly brocade. An inquisitive boy's smile lay on his features," recalled Harrer in his book, that was later made into a film starring Brad Pitt. The meeting led to an unusual friendship. The young Dalai Lama requested the explorer to stay with him as a tutor. Harrer felt honored, agreed—and got to know a young man who loved ice-skating, enjoyed dismantling radios, filmed the city from the roof of Potala Palace, tinkered with his predecessor's automobiles, and announced with childlike pride that the highest mountain in the world lay in his country.

Harrer was much in demand as a messenger from a distant world, as an English and geography teacher, as a

photographer—and as proprietor of a little cinema he had installed at the palace for the Dalai Lama. At times he even lived in the Tibetan winter residence, and noted, "Life in this religious fortress resembles, one supposes, that of a medieval castle. Hardly any object belongs to the present day. In the evening all the gates are closed under the supervision of the Treasurer, after which watchmen go through the whole Palace to see that everything is in order." Harrer witnessed festivities in honor of the divine monarchy. But he also experienced its demise.

After troops of the People's Republic of China invaded Tibet, the Dalai Lama, now fifteen, decided to flee. It was the night of December 19, 1950. Reportedly, the cold winter stars gleamed as the Dalai Lama left the palace at about two in the morning. Ten miles outside Lhasa he apparently descended from the palanquin and looked back at Potala Palace, which was just illuminated by the first rays of the morning sun. As his questions revealed, it appears that did not know where the journey would lead.

1 The golden rooftops of the palace
2 Potala Palace has been the winter residence of the Dalai Lama ever since the 17th century
3 The annual relocation from the summer residence to Potala Palace
4 Potala Palace at daybreak

1

He did not share his brother Philip's love of make-up, jewelry, and expensive clothes. He did, however, enjoy making memorable public appearances. Louis, later King Louis XIV (1638–1715), was an enthusiastic singer, actor, and dancer. In 1653, at age fifteen, he embodied the Greek sun god Apollo in a performance of the *Ballet de la Nuit* at the Petit-Bourbon Palace in Paris. His costume was made of shiny golden material, his face concealed behind a golden mask, and even his hair was tinted gold and fashioned into rays with the aid of sugar water. It was no coincidence that Louis began to enjoy this role all the more when he assumed the throne as king of France. "The sun," he declared, "is the most vital and loveliest symbol of a great prince. For it is unique in its nature and glory, dispensing light and welfare, awaken-

*Versailles! It is wonderfully beautiful! You gaze, and stare, and try to understand that it is real, that it is on the earth, that it is not the Garden of Eden—but your brain grows giddy, stupified by the world of beauty around you, and you half believe you are the dupe of an exquisite dream ... I used to abuse Louis XIV for spending two hundred millions of dollars in creating this marvellous park, when bread was so scarce with some of his subjects, but I have forgiven him now.*

Mark Twain, *The Innocents Abroad*, 1869

VERSAILLES PALACE
France, Versailles, 1661–1710
Architects: Louis Le Vau,
Jules Hardouin-Mansart, and
Robert de Cotte

ing life, joy, and enthusiasm, and is continually in motion despite its appearing to hover in absolute peace."

In Paris, however, this peace seemed threatened. The capital on the Seine was increasingly becoming a nest of subversives. So Louis XIV thought it advisable to shift the seat of government to the country. A site was soon decided upon—a swampy area about twenty kilometers northwest of Paris. Beginning in the year 1661, in the course of several "campaigns," there emerged the largest and most splendid palatial complex in Europe: Versailles Palace. To house 15,000 members of the court, 10,000

laborers worked at the site round the clock. Many were killed or maimed in accidents. "Every night," a lady of the court reported, "they carried away whole cartloads of bodies." Up to forty livres were paid as compensation to workers who had lost an arm or a leg; an eye brought sixty.

By 1682 the complex was provisionally finished, and thereafter the royal sun shone only in Versailles. Louis XIV planned his wars here, and kept the noblemen he required for them in a complaisant mood with continual diversions. "Three times a week a comedy was performed, and every Saturday there was a ball," recounted a contemporary. "On the three other days of the week the court gathered at six in the evening in the Grand Apartment of Louis XIV. There one could converse, listen to the performances of singers and instrumentalists, or dance. The king himself preferred to play billiards."

The rigorous, unchanging rhythms of court etiquette followed the course of the sun. When the king's bedroom was illuminated by its first rays, his morning *lever* began, and when it vanished behind the horizon, everything was made ready for his *coucher*. At his final morning rising, however, Louis XIV, the Sun of France, was no longer conscious. He died on September 1, 1715, shortly after eight in the morning—on a Sunday, like his birthday. On his deathbed he was still able to warn his great-grandson and successor against attempting to follow in his footsteps. He had "loved war too much," Louis admitted, and above all he had "made too great expenditures."

1  Louis XIV in a regal pose, oil painting by Hyacinthe Rigaud, 1701
2  The construction of the palace, painting by Adam-Frans van der Meulen, 1669
3  View of Versailles Palace and its gardens, painting by Pierre Patel, 1668
4  The Versailles Palace, the backdrop for the Sun King Louis XIV's own mise-en-scène
5  The Pool d'Apollon in the park at Versailles
6  The Hall of Mirrors

2

3

4

5

6

# DROTTNINGHOLM PALACE Lake Mälar

DROTTNINGHOLM PALACE
Sweden, Lake Mälar,
1662–1700
Architects: Nicodemus Tessin
the Elder, Nicodemus Tessin
the Younger, et al.

The theater, the opera, and ballet were his world, and if he had ever had the choice, he would have become an actor. Gustav III (1746–92), however, already occupied the Swedish throne at the age of twenty-five, and felt beleaguered by troubles on all sides. The people had rebelled against the traditional order, and the estates demanded power. But the king replied with an iron hand and even managed the amazing feat of consolidating his power in such uncertain times. It was terribly tiring though, and required regular recuperation. So, when summer came, the king would retire to Drottningholm.

The "most joyful palace in Sweden" lies on the island of Lovön in Lake Mälar, and is best reached by ferry from Stockholm. Today the route is plied by a vintage steamer that dates from around 1900. Gustav III, in his day, had himself ferried over in an opulent bark, and enjoyed his weeks on the "island of the blessed" to the full.

Drottningholm is known not only for its Blue Bedroom with its elaborately decorated four-poster bed, but also for its library, with gilt book backs from floor to ceiling. The castle park provided diversions of another kind. On mild summer nights, the charming Chinese Pavilion with its exotic figurines, vases, and silk wall coverings saw

*Drottningholm is a joyful place and this is reflected in its surroundings. There is the bay of Lake Mälar bordering on to the beautiful park; there is the "dancing" of its many fountains, as well as thousands of red tulips shisning along its paths in springtime. Let's not forget the little open-air stage, surrounded by high hedges, which conceals the place where elves, fairies and kobolds dwell, who on a bright midsummer night might too wish to perform a play.*

Bengt Paul, *Drottningholm*, 1971

Gustav III dining with a small party of confidantes. After every course, he would press a button and the table would descend through the floor. Below the kitchen boys waited, ready to clear the table, reset it, and, by turning a crank, would send it up with new delicacies.

If this illustrates the king's fascination with mechanical gadgetry, the palace theater, a freestanding building near the palace, emphasize it even further. Its eighteenth-century machinery, still in perfect working order, was conceived and constructed by a brilliant mechanical engineer from Italy. Among the most significant of its kind in Europe, no other historical theater north of the Alps has been preserved so unchanged through the centuries.

Many features date as far back as the days of Gustav III—wind and wave-making machines, thunder apparatus, portable clouds, and great petroleum lamps with slip frames for colored glass lenses, the predecessors of modern spotlights. But probably the most valuable part of the legacy consists in over thirty largely complete stage sets, in which Gustav III himself appeared as an actor. He had never forgotten his original professional wish. Once he reportedly learned 2,456 lines of verse and over 1,000 lines of prose within the space of a few weeks, in order to act in several plays and roles during his summer stay at Drottningholm. Sometimes he even directed.

The courtiers politely applauded, but his political opponents scoffed at Gustav's passion. Well-meaning friends advised him to "doff the comedian's cloak," or risk general ridicule, which he finally did. That he would nevertheless live on as a stage figure, he could not have suspected. His end was tragic enough to provide good material for a show. On March 29, 1792, at a costume ball at the Stockholm Opera House, the king fell victim to an assassin's pistol. This event inspired the French author Eugène Scribe to write a drama, which served the composer Giuseppe Verdi as the basis for his opera *A Masquerade Ball*, premiered in 1859.

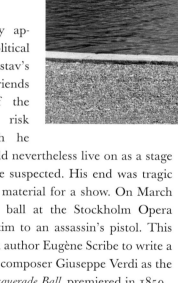

1 Gustav III, painting by A. Roslin
2 The garden facade of the palace
3 The backdrop in the palace theater
4 The Swedish royal family moved back into the palace in 1981

2

3    4

# NYMPHENBURG PALACE Munich

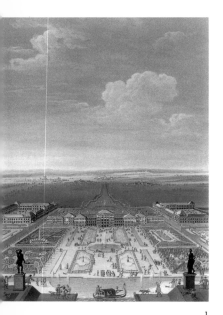

The entire land was elated. After over ten years of marriage, Henriette Adelaide of Bavaria had finally given birth to an heir to the throne. Little Max Emanuel's proud father, Elector Ferdinand Maria, could hardly believe his luck. Such was the gratitude he felt for his "beloved spouse and young mother" that he presented her with extensive properties outside the gates of his capital, Munich, for a new summer palace. But his wife, a daughter of the Duke of Savoy, who had grown up in Turin, received the gift capriciously. Although a new palace would be wonderful, she said, Bavarian architects were "più idioti nell' edificare," great idiots when it came to building. So the planning was entrusted with an Italian, Agostino Barelli of Bologna. Based on his sketches, a mighty pavilion was erected, the central structure of today's palace. Henriette Adelaide christened it Borgo delle Ninfe, Palace of the Nymphs—Nymphenburg.

*When guests arrived from town in long horse-drawn carriages,*
*all Nymphenburg was resplendent with faery illumination.*
*The lines of carriages crossed in front of the cascade,*
*allowing the ladies and gentlemen to watch the play of water.*
*Then they were invited into the palace—to a soupé en public*
*with music in the Great Hall.*

Pierre de Brétagne, *Entertainments and Festivities*
*at Max Emanuel's Court*, Munich, 1723

Max Emanuel, son and heir, lost his mother at age fourteen and his father three years later. He soon found Nymphenburg, his "pleasure house," too small. Congenitally self-assured and celebrated as a swashbuckling twenty-one-year-old commander in the war against the Ottoman Turks, he envisaged nothing less than eclipsing the glory of the Sun King, Louis XIV of France, and becoming emperor himself. Literally building a foundation for this vision, Max Emanuel had a half-dozen palaces erected in the environs of Munich and expanded Nymphenburg into one of the largest palatial complexes in Europe. Hundreds of Turkish prisoners of war reputedly dug the canals along which the Elector and his guests were rowed through the park in Venetian gondolas, to the strains of the court orchestra, as fireworks turned the night sky to day. Although the state coffers had long been emptied and his dream of imperial rule had faded, Max Emanuel continued building.

One of his most original creations in Nymphenburg Palace park was the Badenburg—a sort of sacred spring dedicated to the nymphs, complete with one of the first indoor heated swimming pools in Europe. Pierre de Brétagne, Max Emanuel's father confessor, extolled the

NYMPHENBURG PALACE
Germany, Munich, 1664–1779
Architects: Agostino Barelli,
Enrico Zuccalli, Joseph Effner,
et al.

Badenburg as a "true masterpiece of art, and as regards the purpose for which it was built, the most comfortable place in the world." The court official, however, was literally up to his neck in water by this time. When Max Emanuel died in 1726, he left debts amounting to twenty-six million guilders—seven times the annual tax revenues of the Bavarian state.

1  View from the palace and the canal stretching towards the center of Munich, from a painting by Franz Joachim Beich, c. 1722
2  Nymphenburg Palace seen from the east
3  The Badenburg with its multistory bathroom
4  Cascades and classical sculptures in the palace park

3

4

## When Calm Settled over the Palace

# HET LOO    Apeldoorn

1

HET LOO
The Netherlands, Apeldoorn,
1686–99
Architects: Jacob Roman and
Daniel Marot

When Het Loo looked like a Boy Scout camp and no bed remained unoccupied, Wilhelmina, Queen of The Netherlands (1880–1962), was in her element. Only one worry remained—whether her youthful guests would leave the table hungry. "I'll have a bone to pick with you if any of these children don't get enough," she used to warn the staff in advance of such invitations. The queen, who identified with her role of "mother of the nation" so strongly that people said she preferred brandishing a cooking spoon to a scepter, was renowned for her popularity— and resoluteness. As Winston Churchill once admitted, she was the only woman he feared.

Those associated with her fared no better, and even ministers of state sometimes felt like schoolboys when she rebuked them. Nothing escaped Wilhelmina, and she was quite capable of raising her voice—which the pious protestant often later regretted. "That was not exactly in conformance with the Sermon on the Mount," she used to say in such cases. In fact, she was probably much more sensitive than outward appearances would suggest. At

*How Het Loo lay there yesterday evening, in unprecedented abandonment, with its lanterns shining for no one, its guard posts with more to protect, its locked gates and unlighted windows behind which there is no more life. Everything seems so empty and quiet. With Queen Wilhelmina, its last inhabitant, the palace died, too.*

Thijs Booy, *It Is Now Quiet at Het Loo Palace:
Observations in Memory of Queen Wilhelmina of The Netherlands,* 1964

Het Loo, for instance, whenever a thunderstorm threatened, she would quickly rush to the shelter of her private apartments and hide from the storm.

The Dutch royal family's summer residence northwest of Apeldoorn was Wilhelmina's favorite place. The luxuriously furnished rooms had not only seen the happiest days of her childhood, as boxes of toys and her old hobby-horse recalled, but she had also spent her honeymoon there. And in the park still stood the miniature garden house her father had built for her. No wonder Wilhelmina retired here in 1948, when she relinquished the throne in favor of her daughter, Juliane. The "Palace in the Woods," surrounded by extensive hunting grounds, was her true home, and she found the best painting motifs just a stone's throw away. In the stables at Het Loo one can still see the famous "little painting cart" in which the queen had herself driven through the park, equipped with oil paints and easel, ready to capture on canvas meadows sparkling with wildflowers, windblown copses, or bizarre cloud formations.

Although she enjoyed the privileges of her position, loved crystal chandeliers and fine china, Wilhelmina was no snob—she used to refer to flattery as "court rabies" or "ermine fever." In 1945, when hunger and need reigned in the war-ravaged land, she gave away her fur coats and had the manicured lawns of Het Loo plowed under for peas, cabbage, and beans to feed the populace.

When Queen Wilhelmina, the last denizen of Het Loo, died in 1962, "she left the palace not as queen but as lady of the house," as her former private secretary wrote. "Her coffin was carried out by ordinary men from the surrounding villages and woods. Even the hearse was accompanied not by court excellencies or government officials, but by the plain people. The rural simplicity was so perfect that plow-horses stood by the roadside to pay her their last respects. She, a great animal lover, would surely have found it touching."

2

3

5

1 Het Loo, engraving from the 18th century
2 The palace's rooms are magnificently furnished
3 The understated elegance of Het Loo
4 From 1686 until 1975 Het loo was the preferred summer
  residence of the Dutch royal family
5 The Baroque garden of the palace with globes representing
  the heavens, Venus, and the earth

4

# *In the Realm of the Housewife*

# SCHÖNBRUNN PALACE  Vienna

SCHÖNBRUNN PALACE
Austria, Vienna 1696–1873
Architects: Johann Bernhard
Fischer von Erlach, Nikolaus
Franz Leonhard Freiherr von
Pacassi, and Johann Aman

Empress Maria Theresa (1717–80) was not only a family woman with an earthy wit, but also a good housekeeper. When she decided to spend the summer months at Schönbrunn Palace, her deceased father's abandoned hunting lodge, she ordered a general cleaning, including "washing all the windows and sanding the floors." Moreover, the roof leaked and the walls were damp—but above all, the imperial family needed more room. For Maria Theresa's marriage with Francis Stephen, Duke of Lorraine was not only happy, but fertile, resulting in sixteen children. And they had to be accommodated, along with their personal servants—the thirteen-year-old heir to the throne alone had thirty-two.

Therefore Schönbrunn was "not only to be repaired, but expanded as well." Although she was thrifty and accordingly dismayed when the royal kitchens charged her 4,000 guilders a year just for parsley, Maria Theresa spared no expense. To the director of the royal building bureau she wrote, "let him realize that something good comes out of this and he should not worry about give or take 20,000 guilders more or less." No sooner said than

*Everything accords with the grandeur of the monarch who resides here. The building is magnificent, the furnishings imperial, and in the finest taste. The interior is shown to every stranger, whenever the monarch is not present. Anyone who is interested should apply to the palace captain.*

Johann Edler von Kurzböck, *Latest Description of All the Interesting Sites of Vienna*, 1779

done. After just a year of conversion work, the former hunting lodge had been transformed into a glorious residence with 1,400 rooms. Even members of the imperial family had a hand at decorating the interiors of the palace. The blue ink drawings on the walls of the Porcelain Room and the watercolors in the Miniature Cabinet are the work of Emperor Francis Stephen and three of his daughters.

Domestic bliss reigned at Schönbrunn Palace, as Maria Theresa relaxed court etiquette for the sake of her children. She concerned herself with family matters, helped with the gardening, and never refused a game of backgammon or chess. Still, she did not lose sight of her duties as a monarch. There the "First Lady of Europe" received ministers and generals, diplomats and crowned heads, poets and philosophers—and the six-and-one-half-year-old Wolfgang Amadeus Mozart. On October 13, 1762, the celebrated child prodigy played in the Hall of Mirrors for Maria Theresa, and immediately lost his heart to her: "Wolfgang jumped straight from the harpsichord into her lap, embraced her and smothered her with kisses," reported his father, Leopold, who was reputedly quite shocked by the scene. But Maria Theresa just laughed and said, "Let him be, he only means well. I know all about youngsters, having plenty of them myself!"

1　The "Gloriette"—an elaborate folly in the palace park
2　Garden facade
3　Palm house in the palace park
4　Schönbrunn Palace, painting by Bernardo Bellotto, named Canaletto, c. 1760
5　*Emperor Francis I and Maria Theresa with Their Family*, painting by Martin van Meytens, c. 1754–55
6　The Great Gallery

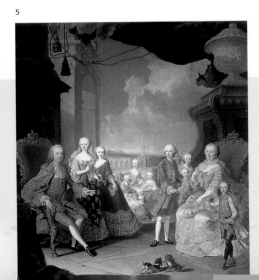

# BELVEDERE PALACE Vienna

*Residence of the Covert Emperor*

# BELVEDERE PALACE  Vienna

His father had reputedly been poisoned, and his mother, it was rumored, had had a hand in it. Nor were the fates particularly kind in other respects to the young Eugene of Savoy (1663–1736). His relatives looked upon the deformed prince with his too long chin and short upper lip as "a slovenly fellow who gave no hope of doing or becoming anything." Not even his grandmother liked him. When he resisted her orders to go into the priesthood and decided on an officer's career instead, she cut off his allowance. But the French army would not have him, either—because he wasn't tall enough.

So in 1683, nineteen years old and penniless, Prince Eugene arrived in Vienna. The Turks stood at the gates of the Habsburg capital and royal residence, and the

> *When one drives to the border of the city, one sees a magnificent edifice that outshines all the other palaces in, and outside, Vienna. This is the incomparable palace of Prince Eugene of Savoy, the greatest hero of our times. The view of the city from here is dreamlike, and can be especially enjoyed when one is riding in one of the little gondolas on the grand water basin.*
>
> After Johann Basilius Küchelbecker, *The Latest News of the Roman Imperial Court,*
> *Supplemented by a Detailed Historical Description of the Residence City of Vienna,* 1730

imperial troops needed every man they could get. The "foreign prince" was immediately put in uniform—and began a breathtaking career. By the time he was twenty, Eugene had become regimental commander, at thirty he was a field marshal, at forty he became president of the court war council, and as such the most important minister in the Habsburg empire. Each new post brought a raise in salary, supplemented by the generous gifts of money, which the emperor bestowed on his ablest subject.

Finally Prince Eugene, now revered as "the noble knight," "covert emperor," and "creator of the great power of Austria," commissioned the renowned Lukas von Hildebrandt to build him a summer residence that could bear comparison to any of the Habsburgers' magnificent edifices. Although his relatives were green with envy, encouragement came from Montesquieu. It was a wonderful feeling, the eminent French author said, to spend time in a country where the subjects lived in a much more noble manner than the imperial family themselves.

Guests invited to the prince's opulent receptions and pampered by servants in Turkish costume with "confectionery, fruit creations, coffee, and lemonade" were likewise enthusiastic: "Nothing is finer than a gathering in the palace of this prince," wrote one contemporary. "Then the cour d'honneur and gardens are illuminated by countless lanterns, as if by a magic wand."

Equally renowned were Eugene's gallery of paintings, library, and porcelain collection. Another source of wonder was his menagerie, particularly when, to his guests' horror, one of his tame lions suddenly appeared at the table. His collection of rare animals was even rumored to include a "double eagle"—a legend Prince Eugene used to greet with a smile, but, probably in deference to his nation's symbol, never denied.

After his death most of the animals ended up in the circus. His other valuable possessions, too, were sold and scattered to the winds—by a niece who had been declared heiress. Eugene of Savoy left no direct heirs. He had never married, because for an army man, a wife was apparently merely a "bothersome piece of furniture" who would only prevent her beloved husband from fighting to the hilt.

UPPER AND LOWER BELVEDERE
Austria, Belvedere Palace, Vienna,
1700–24
Architect: Lukas von Hildebrandt

1  The palace's main entrance facade
2  *Prince Eugene's Gardens in Belvedere,* engraving by J. A. Corvinus
3  Portrait of Prince Eugene by an unknown painter
4  *Prince Eugene's Menagerie,* by Salomon Kleiner, 1734
5  The palace's garden side
6  View of the park between the upper and lower Belvederes
7  The Sala terrena on the ground floor

5

6

7

# BUCKINGHAM PALACE   London

BUCKINGHAM PALACE
England, London, 1703–1913
Architects: John Nash, Edward
Blore, et al.

A love of dogs runs in the family. It was already said that Queen Victoria, having returned to Buckingham Palace from her coronation in Westminster Abbey, had nothing more urgent to do than roll up her sleeves and bathe her favorite spaniel, Daisy. Her passion is matched by Queen Elizabeth II, who dotes on her Welsh corgis with the same delight. She also breeds Labrador retrievers, and gives them such honeyed names as Sandringham Slipper or Sherry of Biteabout. But the history of Buckingham Palace is not, of course, only about dogs.

The palace began as the comparatively humble country house of the Duke of Buckingham. Back then the region was still quite swampy. It was not until the ground had been drained, the clay layer removed and baked into bricks, that construction sites were obtained for what became today's posh neighborhood of Belgravia. Concurrently, the old country house, which had since passed to the royal family, was expanded and converted into a

> *Buckingham Palace, the present residence of the queen, is not quite so ugly as St. James, the old royal castle, which looks like a caricature of itself. Yet one cannot say that Buckingham Palace is that much more beautiful. At any rate, it does not succeed in erasing the boredom that stands written on its brow.*
>
> Theodor Fontane, *A Summer in London*, 1854

luxurious residence. Queen Victoria was the first regent to make Buckingham Palace, with its cool magnificence, her London residence and seat of government. Ever since, it has figured as *the* symbol of British monarchy. The palace doors, however, remained closed to the subjects who, in the nineteenth century already, marveled at the colorful daily ceremony of the changing of the guards.

This has since changed. The monarchy has attempted to compensate for the loss of face it suffered in the past due to homemade scandals, by becoming more transparent. Since 1993, for the first time in its history, Buckingham Palace has been open to the public—if only during the summer months. That only nineteen of the total of six hundred rooms may be viewed, is not really a disadvantage. On display next door, are not only the royal Bentleys and Rolls Royces, but the magnificent state carriage from the period of George III, whose suspension, notorious for inducing motion sickness, was fitted with new shock absorbers at the behest of Queen Elizabeth II.

In 2002, something unheard-of happened—on the occasion of her Golden Coronation Jubilee, the queen sent out invitations to a pop music concert in the Buckingham Palace garden. She seems not to have been entirely comfortable with the decision. The stars who were to perform, including Elton John, Paul McCartney, and Tom Jones, were sent an etiquette list in advance. The rules prohibited wearing shorts, baring chests, shouting, drug taking, and digging holes in the lawn. The musicians obliged. Still, Elizabeth II found a reason not to be amused. The rock version of *God Save the Queen*, performed by the former Queen guitarist Brian May standing on the roof of Buckingham Palace, reportedly left her rather cold.

1  The palace gates
2  *Buckingham Palace*, watercolor by John Nash, 1846
3  The main facade of Buckingham Palace
4  The changing of the guards takes place every day at 11:30 A.M.

2

3

4

It was Good Friday of the year 1701. Worshippers in the churches of the Saxon residence of Dresden were remembering the sufferings of Christ when suddenly the fire bells rang out—the palace was in flames! From the attic of King George's building the conflagration spread through several tracts and floors, destroyed the soaring wooden roof structure of the Great Hall, and then, when the firehoses began to take effect, died out just short of the apartments of Augustus the Strong. The Saxon Elector, for four years now king of Poland as well, was far from the Elbe River on that day, and when informed of the disaster in a dispatch, he seemed surprisingly unmoved.

Having long felt confined in his ancestors' palace, Augustus viewed the fire as a welcome opportunity to tear down what remained of the old edifice and erect a new, extensive and truly royal residence in its place.

*In Dresden ... all inventions of the building arts mingle in a most agreeable way. Quite incomparable, however, is the Zwinger. The least one can say about this so superbly designed pleasure garden is, that it is justifiably called an earthly paradise—especially on account of its exceedingly splendid building style. It would not be easy to find anything more beautiful in the world.*

Johann Michael von Loen, *Sylvander's von Edel-Leben Occasional Observations*, 1726

THE ZWINGER
Germany, Dresden, 1709–32
Architect: Matthäus Daniel
Pöppelmann
Sculptor of figurative ornament: Balthasar Permoser

Only a part of his opulent vision, however, would be realized: the Zwinger. Strictly speaking, this building is little more than a fairground, bordered by galleries and pavilions in orangery style, the "Bath of the Nymphs"

and the "Crown Gate." Yet the ebullient playfulness of its architecture and the abundance of its figurative ornament make the Zwinger one of the most original buildings of its era.

The first great celebration held here marked the marriage of Elector Frederick Augustus of Saxony and Maria Anna, daughter of the emperor. On September 20, 1719, the groom's father, Augustus the Strong, presented a "Fair of the Nations," with harlequinades, musicians and rope dancers, sideshows, Italian comedies, marionette theaters, and a lottery. Stages and a Turkish serai had been set up in the inner court, and long tables in the provisionally finished pavilions groaned under the weight of all sorts of delicacies. Most of the guests came in costume, and Augustus the Strong reveled in his role of host—as if embodying the sustainer of his land, spreading abundance and oblivious of the existence of need.

Many festivities were celebrated here, but soon the boisterousness subsided. In 1729, the Zwinger was transformed from a "festival backdrop in stone" into a *Palais Royale des Sciences*—a repository for the princely and royal collections. It was Augustus the Strong himself who issued the decree in 1728: "I desire that my library, all valuables and antiques, the animals, the natural objects and insects, the medallions, the engravings and herbal books, the anatomy chamber and all of the appurtenances relating to astronomy, surgery, mathematics, physics, etc., as well as all other curiosities, now be brought to the Zwinger." These treasures were open to public view, in exchange for a four-guilder fee.

The collections are still very much worth a visit today. Their treasures include not only an Arabian celestial globe from the thirteenth century, but also the oldest calculator in the world, developed in 1642 by Blaise Pascal.

2

3

4

5

1 Herm pillar in the Wallpavillon
2 Portrait of Augustus the Strong, founder of the Baroque city of Dresden, engraving by Johann Martin Bernigeroth
3 The Elector's palace in Dresden before the great fire, engraving by A. Weck, 1680
4 The Zwinger, the symbol of Dresden
5 The "Bath of the Nymphs"

# CATHERINE'S PALACE near St. Petersburg

1

Today the small town is called Pushkin, after the great Russian poet who went to school at the exclusive Alexander Lyceum in the palace park and later owned a *dacha*, a summer cottage, nearby. Back then, the vacation spot outside the capital, St. Petersburg, was known as Tsarskoye Selo, or Village of the Czars, due to the frequency with which Russian rulers went there for rest and recreation. From 1837 onwards it was the last stop on Russia's first railroad line, built from St. Petersburg.

The czars' favorite family seat was a little world in its own right, and incredibly magnificent. Catherine's Palace with its 325-meter-long facade, extolled at the time as a "Baroque ocean of sky-blue walls and white columns," is still considered one of the most superb examples of European palatial architecture.

*When the weather was fine, the czar and his children interrupted their work at eleven sharp each morning to take the fresh air for an hour. Sometimes they clambered into little rowboats and cruised along the canals of Tsarskoje Selo. In wintertime they amused themselves by shoveling snow, building forts, and sledding in the park.*

Anna Virubova, *Memoirs of Life at the Court of Czar Nicholas II*, 1923

CATHERINE'S PALACE
Russia, near St.Petersburg,
1718–24
refurbished 1752–7
Architect: Bartolomeo
Francesco Rastrelli

Among its most exquisite chambers was the fabled "eighth wonder of the world," an unprecedented interior whose disappearance in 1941 has become a myth of recent history: the Amber Room. In the warm glow of its candlelit panels, Catherine the Great is said to have whiled away long dark winter evenings playing cards.

Recreation was also the aim of the 1,500-acre park with its artificial ruins, pavilions, teahouses, oriental baths, a Dutch dairy, and a Chinese hamlet. On the canals

bobbed Taiwanese junks, Brazilian fishing boats, and a whole fleet of miniature galleys. Among the trees, grouped with the care of a stage backdrop, shone columns and obelisks commemorating the Russian victory over the Turks—or the passing away of one of the czar's children's pet rabbits. The Romanovs, who ruled Russia from 1682 onwards, were unusually fond of animals. Nicholas II, born in 1868 in Tsarskoje Selo and the last czar of the enormous empire, was no exception. As often as his duties permitted, he would roam the park with his eleven Scottish shepherd dogs. The favorite pet of his son, the czarevitch, on the other hand, was a great gray cat, who slept in the successor's bed and comforted him in his fight against leukemia.

By that time, however, the family had long since left Catherine's Palace, which was used only on ceremonial occasions and—during World War I—as a military hospital. Nicholas II had had the considerably more modest Alexander's Palace, in a distant corner of the park, furnished as a domicile for himself and his loved ones. It was from here that the czar's family would leave on their final journey. Following the bloody demise of the monarchy, they were put under house arrest in Tsarskoje Selo, and around five o'clock one morning, were picked up, never to return. On July 16, 1918, Nicholas II, his German-born wife Alexandra, and their five children died in a hail of bullets from a Bolshevist firing squad in Yekaterinburg.

1 The palace gates
2 Czar Nicholas II with his son Alexander shoveling snow in Tsarskoye Selo
3 The "Baroque ocean," the facade of Catherine's Palace
4 The Amber Room, reconstruction completed in 2003

2

3

4

# THE WÜRZBURG RESIDENCE Würzburg

It was scandalous. For years the court high chamberlain of the Princely Diocese of Würzburg had clandestinely diverted considerable sums of money into his own pocket. But it finally came out—in front of a judge. The miscreant was required to repay the embezzled funds in their entirety. To Johann Philipp Franz von Schönborn, Prince Bishop of Würzburg, the money—500,000 guilders, equivalent to about 30 million dollars today—must have seemed a godsend. Since he always had a tendency to extravagance, he immediately knew that he would invest it in the construction of a new residence.

His family reacted skeptically. "The good Lips," as Johann Philipp Franz was known to his relatives, had no experience in building matters, was a dilettante, and moreover had no taste whatsoever. So his entire clan

*The princes had become gods. And temples were erected to them. One of the most magnificent was from the hand of Balthasar Neumann. In order to provide a haven for happiness, the arts in Würzburg lavishly assisted. Tiepolo extended the Venetian sky over the stairwell, the park with its little stone urchins, the wrought iron portals— these are the splendors of a paradise on earth.*

After Ricarda Huch, *In the Old Empire, Pictures from the Life of German Cities*, 1926

WÜRZBURG RESIDENCE
Germany, Würzburg, 1720–44
Decorations begun in 1750 by
Giovanni Battista Tiepolo
Architect: Balthasar Neumann

plunged themselves into the planning process, not facilitating it in the least. They defended their ideas tooth and claw, as if they were a matter of faith. That the family was finally able to agree on a result, was due only to the supervision of the entire process, by the architect Balthasar Neumann. He compiled the best ideas and, with a sure hand, blended them into what would become one of the artistically most significant palatial complexes in Europe.

Even Napoleon enthused, declaring the Würzburg Residence "the loveliest parsonage in the world." Its most daring feature was likely the stairwell, whose enormous ceiling arched across the space without intervening supports—which soon raised doubts as to its stability. One

scoffer even offered to "hang himself under the vault at his own expense," presuming it would not hold his weight. But Neumann was unimpressed. A whole battery of cannons could be fired off in the stairwell, he insisted, and not even an impact of such force would put so much as a crack in the ceiling.

Yet the stairwell was not only a brilliant architectural coup; it contained a stroke of artistic genius. It is overarched by the largest ceiling fresco in the world, an Allegory of the Four Continents, occupying an area of about 600 square meters. Its author was Giovanni Battista Tiepolo, the grand master of Venetian art. Tiepolo arrived in Würzburg on December 12, 1750, and prepared to decorate the residence together with his sons, Domenico and Lorenzo. The result, congenially supplementing Neumann's architecture, is an interdisciplinary work of art of the highest order.

Tiepolo not only depicted himself in the ceiling fresco, but his architectural colleague as well—clad in uniform and flanked by cannons. The latter were intended to recall that Balthasar Neumann was not originally an architect but a master in the casting of heavy guns.

1 The Würzburg Residence, drawing by Sebastian Vierheilig,
  c. 1805
2 The garden front of the Residence
3 The architect Balthasar Neumann in Tiepolo's ceiling fresco
4 The landing of the monumental Grand Staircase and the ceiling
  fresco by Giovanni Battista Tiepolo

# ESTERHÁZA PALACE near Fertöd

Music ran in the Esterházys' blood. For generations, the sons and daughters of the respected Hungarian family learned to play musical instruments. Prince Nicholas Esterházy (1714–90), the Habsburg field marshal, devoted himself to chamber music. He played the cello, the viola, and a cumbersome and therefore justly forgotten string instrument known as the baryton. Yet despite his musical passion, Prince Nicholas was said to be terribly untalented. The entire court whispered about the dissonant dilettantism of their otherwise so respected master. They found all the more pleasure in the organ playing and conducting of a gifted musician who was already being celebrated as a master of perfect harmonies: Joseph Haydn.

The famous composer, who had once moved from tavern to tavern playing the fiddle at dances, in 1766 became chief conductor at Esterháza Palace, a post he would hold for twenty-four years. Nicholas was at least capable of recognizing quality when he saw it, as he had proven once before. During a visit to Versailles he was so overcome by the Sun King's opulence that he decided to emulate it back home, in Hungary. The proud possessor of 140,000 acres of land, Nicholas did not lack the wherewithal to expand his old family seat near Fertöd into a monumental palace in the French style.

Esterháza was equipped with an opera stage, and first-class singers and instrumentalists were hired to bring it to life. This was Haydn's responsibility, as was insuring the pristine whiteness of his troupe's stockings and the proper fit of their wigs. Meanwhile, Haydn composed dozens of sonatas, string quartets, masses, and other works at Esterháza. But above all he wrote operas, whose performance at the palace brought him his greatest triumphs. The Palace became a widely renowned haven of the muses. Even Empress Maria Theresa was deeply impressed. After attending a performance of Haydn's *L'Infedeltà Delusa* as Prince Nicolas' guest in September 1773, she exclaimed, "Anyone who wishes to see a good opera must simply come to Esterháza."

> *On alternate days there are performances of either Italian operas or German comedies, always attended by the prince. The delight to eye and ear is indescribable when the entire orchestra resounds and the soul is suffused, now by the most moving delicacy, now by the most extreme force of the instruments—for the great composer, Joseph Haydn, conducts in person.*
>
> Anonymous, *Description of the Most Princely Palace of Esterháza in the Kingdom of Hungary*, 1784

1 The palace gates
2 Portrait of the composer Joseph Haydn, copy of a painting by Ludwig Guttenbrunn, c. 1770
3 Music of the *Farewell Symphony*, composed by Joseph Haydn at Esterháza Palace in 1772
4 The garden facade
5 Aerial view of the palace complex

ESTERHÁZA PALACE
Hungary, near Fertöd,
1720–67
Architects: Anton Erhard
Martinelli, and Melchior
Hefele

2

3

4

5

## A Masterpiece of Illusion

# STUPINIGI PALACE near Turin

1

He did not appreciate poets. "They only waste paper," Charles Emanuel II (1701–73), Duke of Savoy and King of Sardinia, reputedly said of writers. Nor was he always comfortable around art. Pictures in which he discovered heroes or gods in innocent nakedness were immediately ordered burned by the bigoted monarch, or so the story goes. But architecture was perceived entirely differently. Charles Emanuel dreamed of a magnificent residence, a place of "pleasant diversion and refined conversation"— a heartfelt wish shared by his German-born wife, Polyxena-Christina of Hesse, who reveled in balls, receptions, illuminations, and festive dinners.

The prospective location of the palace was not an issue. Charles Emanuel's father, tired of office after fifty-four years of rule and concerned about his "fluctuating

*Coming from Turin, a magnificent boulevard leads to the palace. The dimensions of the stately edifice are enormous, the arrangement of its tracts truly bizarre. Nevertheless, Stupinigi achieves a very pleasant effect. That it is a hunting seat is indicated by the colossal bronze stag topping the roof. Located directly behind it is the festival hall, doubtless the biggest surprise in this wonderful palace. Here the wildest architect's dreams have come true. The room is a masterpiece of illusion, a utopia, a fantastic theater stage.*

J.J. Lalande, *A Frenchman's Journey to Italy,* 1769

STUPINIGI PALACE
Italy, near Turin, 1729–89
Architects: Filippo Juvarra,
Benedetto Alfieri, et al.

health," abdicated and left the couple a building site outside the gates of Turin. The first walls of a new residence had already gone up. Partridges, storks, and sandpipers abounded, and at twilight foxes, hares, deer, and wild boar emerged out of the thicket—the swampy area had been the favorite hunting grounds of the dukes of Savoy for centuries. Then it became the site of one of the most impressive specimens of palatial architecture, Stupinigi.

Contemporaries had already enthused about the extravagant plan of the massive complex, resembling the Greek letter omega ($\Omega$). Its hexagonal honor court, which issued in a broad poplar-lined drive, opened out like an amphitheater to the northeast. And anyone who approached the palace from that direction must have felt they were facing an enormous stage with serried sets that drew the eye ever farther into the distance—until brought up short by the stage backdrop. But the surprises did not end there. The festival hall, heart of the whole complex, was built on the plan of a St. Andrew's cross, and with its high ceiling, circumambient gallery, and gathered curtains gave the impression of a theater space in its own right.

The first spectacle to play itself out here, however, was unplanned. In 1766, when the superb bronze stag was hoisted onto the roof ridge, the rafters proved incapable of bearing its weight. The sculpture crashed through the roof, taking the ceiling mural down with it. So it took a bit longer before the true opening could be celebrated at Stupinigi—in autumn 1773, when Princess Maria Theresa of Savoy and Sardinia wed the later King Charles X of France in the presence of the European high aristocracy. The festival hall was fantastically decorated, and the palace's facades magically illuminated by thousands of torches. Afterwards, in the garden, a great fireworks display was held that lit up the entire Po valley.

Charles Emanuel and his wife were sadly no longer alive to share the experience. Their creation is known by the humble name of *Palazzina di caccia*, or hunting lodge. In fact, Stupinigi is one of the largest palatial complexes in all of Italy.

1 *The Hunt's Begin in the Palace Gardens of Stupinigi,*
 V. A. Cignaroli
2 Stupinigi Palace marks the pinnacle of northern Italian
 palace building in the eighteenth century
3 The richly ornamented festival hall is in the center of the
 palace complex

3 >

# A Will Fulfilled

# SANSSOUCI Potsdam

1

**SANSSOUCI PALACE**
Germany, Potsdam, 1745–47
Architect: Georg Wenzeslaus
von Knobelsdorff

Nowhere did he feel more at home than here. When he happened not to be fighting a war, King Frederick II of Prussia (1712–86) enjoyed most being at Sanssouci, his "pleasure house by the vineyard" beyond the gates of the garrison town of Potsdam. He himself made the first sketches for palace and park, envisaging a "refuge of peace, of domestic life, the beauties of nature, and the muses." This architectural jewel was completed on May 1, 1747.

Far from the din and bloodshed of the battles with which he made Prussia into a great European power, Sanssouci became Frederick's private retreat. He sported with his greyhounds on the terrace and received Casanova in the garden. He debated with Voltaire in the library, and dined with guests of his legendary "round tables" in the Marble Hall. Frederick acquired masterpieces by Rubens and Van Dyck at auction for his Picture Gallery, and played the flute in the Concert Room, accompanied on the spinet by Carl Philipp Emanuel Bach. As talented an author and thinker as he was a musician, Frederick liked to style himself the "philosopher of Sanssouci." But the palace also experienced him as a duty-bound, increasingly tyrannical monarch who insisted on absolute order, cleanliness, and discipline. The only one exempted from these "typical Prussian virtues" was himself. Stooped over with gout, he flailed at servants and ministers with his cane. His coats were threadbare, he never washed except in an emergency, and he flaunted all etiquette.

When "Old Fritz" died at Sanssouci at two in the morning on August 17, 1786, after nearly fifty years of rule, "all was dead quiet," imagined the German author Thomas Mann in a literary reminiscence, "but no one was sad. Since they could find no unmended or clean shirt in his drawers, a servant donated one of his own, in which they clad his body. It was as tiny as a child's." In his last will and testament, Frederick II the Great stipulated that he be buried at Sanssouci. Yet his nephew and successor, Frederick William II, did not respect his childless uncle's wish. Inspecting the sepulcher, the new monarch declared, "this shabby masonry does not conform with the dignity of a king." The sarcophagus was taken to the Garrison Church in Potsdam.

Yet this was not destined to be Frederick's final resting place. In spring 1943, as Allied air raids threatened the church, the sarcophagus was evacuated to the central headquarters of the air force, in Wildpark outside Potsdam. Thus began an unprecedented odyssey. It was not until August 17, 1991, the 205th anniversary of his death, that Frederick the Great's will was finally fulfilled and he returned to Sanssouci. Today the greatest king of Prussia rests on the topmost garden terrace among his most beloved companions, his greyhounds, whom his servants were required to address formally.

> *In the first years of his reign and shortly after the erection of the palace, the king had a sepulcher built on the uppermost garden terrace, which could continually be seen from his apartments. Once, strolling along this terrace with the Marquis d'Argens, the king discussed the future name of the palace with him. The marquis suggested the name Sanssouci. "Not bad," replied the king, but pointing meaningly to his sepulcher he added, "My dear Marquis, only there shall I be free of cares."*
>
> Friedrich Nicolai, *Anecdotes about King Frederick II*, 1789

1 Pavilion in the park (detail)
2 Garden front
3 *A Flute Concert of Frederick the Great at Sanssouci*, painting by Adolph Menzel, 1850–52
4 Drawing by Frederick the Great, with ground plan and terrace layout, 1744
5 View from the park

2

3

4

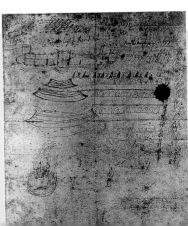

## The Palace on the Lake

# JAG NIWAS     Udaipur

Udaipur has been praised by poets as the "City of the Marble Palaces" and the "Queen of the Lakes." The site of the capital of the former Indian state of Udaipur, today in the southern part of the state of Rajasthan, could hardly in fact be more idyllic. Embedded in the green Aravalli mountain range and filled with gardens of bougainvillea, hibiscus, and roses, the old town with its picturesque lanes nestles along the shores of four artificial lakes. "Udaipur appears so incredible in its beauty that, as usually happens in dreams, I stand in its midst, look, enjoy—and yet can hardly believe what I am experiencing," noted the German traveler and philosopher Hermann Graf Keyserling in 1912.

1

*Here they listened to the tale of the bard, and slept off their noonday opiate amidst the cool breezes of the lake, wafting delicious odours from the myriads of the lotus flower which covered the surface of the waters...*

James Tod, *Annals and Antiquities of Rajasthan or the Central and Western Rajput States*, 1894

The magnificent urban palace, whose facades are beautifully mirrored in the waters of Lake Pichola, is the legacy of the oldest of the twenty-four dynasties of ancient Rajasthan. Here the maharanas of Udaipur resided in unbelievable luxury—down to furniture fashioned of Belgian crystal. The princely residence is not only the most opulent but also the largest palace in Rajasthan, an enormous labyrinth of courtyards, stairways, gardens, terraces, kiosks, galleries, colonnades, and stepped facades that grew from generation to generation. Lack of space, one imagines, would hardly have been a problem.

JAG NIWAS
India, Udaipur, c. 1746–57

Still, as legend has it, in 1746 the reigning maharana, Amar Singh, refused to grant his son's wish to hold a great party in the city palace. If he wanted to amuse himself, declared his father, he should build a palace of his own. The prince, the future Maharana Jagat Singh II, immediately complied. In the middle of Lake Pichola—on a small island barely three hundred meters from the bank on the city side and the impressive backdrop of his father's palace—he erected Jag Niwas, a palace that seems to float above the water like a vision from the *Arabian Nights*. Behind the white walls lie intimate courtyards with softly murmuring fountains, tiny gardens awash with blossoms, chambers with mirrored walls, exquisite painted miniatures, and inlays of marble and colored glass.

Here Prince Jagat Singh celebrated with his retinue, entertained by jugglers, acrobats, snake charmers, and the inevitable bards. His successors appreciated the venue just as much as the young maharana. As late as 1912, according to Graf Keyserling, they still had themselves rowed over to the island in "opulent barks decked out in colored flags, in golden gondolas, and accompanied by singing and the sound of cymbals."

In the twentieth century the island palace was discovered for the movies as well. Fritz Lang made *The Tiger of Eschnapur* in the palace and, in *Octopussy*, James Bond stayed here as an hotel guest in its opulent ambience. Jagat Singh's erstwhile pleasure seat has in fact been used as a noble lodging place for decades. The only shadow that might fall across a stay there would be the memory of a female acrobat who attempted to cross Lake Pichola on a tightrope. If she succeeded, promised the maharana of the time, half of his kingdom would be hers. Just before she reached the shore though, a courtier severed the rope, and the young woman unfortunately drowned. Ever since, they say, her ghost can be seen hovering across the lake on moonlit nights.

2

3

4

1 The City Palace of Udaipur, illustration from *India of Rajahs*, by Louis Rousselet, 1875
2 Jag Niwas was converted into the luxurious Lake Palace Hotel in 1960
3 Jag Niwas, the former palace embedded in the Aravalli Hills and reflected in the waters of Lake Pichola
4 A view of Jag Niwas and the City Palace

# WINTER PALACE  St. Petersburg

Thousands of forced laborers and peasants stood barefoot in the brackish water. With uncovered hands they shoveled mud into willow baskets and lugged it to spots where shores were to be reinforced, plateaus raised, and walls built. It was backbreaking work. Those who did not die of exhaustion were wiped out by dysentery, scurvy, or swamp fever. But Peter the Great (1672–1725), the Russian czar, knew no mercy. At this spot on the Neva Delta at the easternmost end of the Gulf of Finland, he intended to build a bulwark against the Swedes. At the same time he wanted it to be "a window on Europe," as Alexander Pushkin would later write. He succeeded in both respects.

In the face of every obstacle there grew out of the foggy sea marshes and forests the new capital of Russia,

*Over the Neva River stood a huge red sun. The buildings of St. Petersburg seemed to dissolve, turning into evanescent lilac-gray lace. A golden red reflection lay on the windows, the tall towers glittered ruby red while the Winter Palace glowed. Rastrelli was its builder. Back then the palace stood like an azure wall in a swarm of white columns. Suddenly Elizabeth, the czarina, opened the window and gazed over the waters of the Neva.*

Andrei Belyi, *St. Petersburg*, 1959

**WINTER PALACE**
Russia, St. Petersburg,
1754–86
Architects: Bartolomeo
Francesco Rastrelli, et al.

St. Petersburg—the cosmopolitan center of the country and the largest seaport far and wide. Permission to build houses directly on the riverbank was granted only to dockworkers and seamen. This rule applied to the czar as well. Yet since he had trained as a carpenter, he was allowed to settle by the water. The enormous Winter Palace that now stands on the site was a work of his daughter, Czarina Elizabeth Petrovna (1709–62), who had the "Dutch House," where her father died in 1725, torn down.

Filial piety played a much lesser role in Elizabeth's life than a love of luxury. Her wardrobe, comprising over 15,000 gowns and matching accessories, was as much talked about in Paris as in Vienna or Dresden. The fortune she had inherited was said to be fabulous. And when gold ore was discovered in incredible amounts near Yekaterinburg in 1745 and those proceeds too began flowing into the state coffers, Elizabeth lost all sense of moderation. With the erection of the Winter Palace, the most glorious era of the Russian dynasty began.

Yet Elizabeth was no snob. She cursed like a fishwife and went on pilgrimages down dusty country roads alongside ordinary peasant women. She also was a practical soul. During construction of the Winter Palace, she lived with her retinue in a nearby makeshift wooden structure. Yet she was not to experience the termination of her ambitious project.

Catherine the Great (1729–96), Elizabeth's successor, was the first Russian ruler to reside in the Winter Palace. She, in turn, commissioned two side annexes for her private apartments, where she not only entertained emissaries but held brilliant soirées. The superb collection of paintings Catherine amassed here would form the basis of one of the most famous museums in the world: The Hermitage.

What the opulent palace has in common with a humble hermitage is naturally a question that has long been asked, not only by today's two million visitors annually. The French ambassador to Catherine's court, a frequent guest at her convivial parties, declared that in the hermitages he was familiar with he had always missed the overwhelming splendor of Catherine's suites, the quality of the furniture, and the abundance of Old Masters—and even more, the luxurious conservatory, "which here, in the midst of polar ice, simulates an Italian spring."

1 Portrait of *Peter the Great*, painting by Jean Marc Nattier, 1840
2 The palace by night
3 View of the Malachite Hall of Winter Palace
4 The fabulous main facade

# WÖRLITZ PALACE  Wörlitz

1

His grandfather, baron of the empire and Prussian field marshal, had introduced the measured march. His grandson, Francis, did not inherit this military bent. He hung up his officer's jacket at age seventeen; and when he assumed the rule of Anhalt-Dessau a year later, he declared his principality neutral—much to the displeasure of Frederick the Great. The king of Prussia had counted on Francis as a faithful ally in his campaigns. Bitterly disappointed, his reply to Francis was couched in rather unconventinal language: "Your neutrality will agree with you like the dogs that eat grass!"

*The duke lived in Wörlitz by himself and with his private pleasures. He enjoyed seeing himself in the role of the English lord who had retired from government affairs for a few days to enjoy country life. When distinguished visitors came to Wörlitz, a great banquet was held in the palace. Only then did the lord make way for the baron.*

Friedrich Reil, *Duke Francis of Anhalt-Dessau, with Regard to his Activities and Personality,* 1784

WÖRLITZ PALACE
Germany, Wörlitz, 1769–73
Architect: Friedrich Wilhelm
von Erdmannsdorff

Crude language could not sway the philosophically astute Francis. Instead of going to war he set out to expand his horizons by traveling extensively through Europe. Brought up in more of a bourgeois than a courtly atmosphere, Francis was particularly taken with England, where he felt surrounded by a "sense of true human dignity."

The cradle of the Enlightenment, the British kingdom had the most democratic constitution in Europe at that time, and it also led the Continent in terms of technology, architecture, agriculture, and garden design. When he returned home, Francis devoted all his efforts to transforming his small principality into a model land, based on the English example. Every one of his 35,000 subjects had free access to him; he reformed cattle raising and farming, preached tolerance of the Jews, maintained per-

3

sonal contact with Goethe, and introduced universal education. Francis' love of England was also reflected in Wörlitz Palace, with which his friend, the architect Friedrich Wilhelm von Erdmannsdorff, established German Neoclassicism.

Its steam-powered water circulation system, a bathroom that was anything but standard at the time, its elevators, its beds that folded into the wall, were all British inventions that Francis introduced into Germany. Yet the most significant legacy of the enlightened duke was Wörlitz Park, the first English landscape garden on the Continent. It was open to the public and was largely left to its own devices. In England, untrimmed trees and shrubs, in contrast to the manicured, strictly geometric Baroque garden reserved for the nobility, were considered to reflect middle-class freedoms. Yet apparently not even the most enlightened ruler could do without a spectacle—a miniature version of Mount Vesuvius, erected right in the middle of the park. On special occasions Francis would trigger an artificial eruption. Accompanied by loud rumblings, the little volcano began to spit fire, which, in the duke's eyes, symbolized "the Light of Reason."

2

1  English country houses and Italian villas served as models for Wörlitz Palace
2  The library
3  A depiction of Mount Vesuvius' eruption in the park
4  Numerous canals cross the palace park
5  "Here it is tremendously beautiful. I was very moved yesterday, by how the gods have permitted the Prince to create a dream around him," wrote Johann Wolfgang von Goethe on the park at Wörlitz

## *The City of Angels*
# ROYAL PALACE  Bangkok

For two hundred years travelers have been at a loss for new superlatives to describe the palatial city on the left bank of the Chao Phraya River. The residence of Thai kings has been called a "Far Eastern fairy-tale world" or "an orgy in gold, jade, and marble." Apart from the many opulent buildings of the ruling family, "the royal heart of Bangkok" contains over one hundred additional structures: ceremonial halls, temples, pagodas, and pavilions with multicolored stepped roofs and gilded spires, surrounded by bronze lions, frightening guardian figures, bird-men, apes and demons in stone. One of the oldest monuments is known as the Amarinda Hall.

1

*There it was, spread largely on both banks, the Oriental capital… Here and there in the distance, above the crowded mob of low, brown roof ridges, towered great piles of masonry, King's Palace, temples, gorgeous and dilapidated, crumbling under the vertical sunlight, tremendous, overpowering, almost palpable, which seemed to enter one's breast with the breath of one's nostrils and soak into one's limbs through every pore of one's skin.*

Joseph Conrad, *The Shadow-Line: A Confession*, 1917

Here, where Thailand's kings are still crowned, once reigned Rama I. After long consultations with his astrologers, Rama I raised "Bang Makok"—the erstwhile "village of the wild olives"—to the status of capital city on April 6, 1782, and dubbed it "City of Angels." In other words, Bangkok entered history as a royal residence no more than two hundred years ago. Nevertheless, the "Venice of the East," as the city is known for its many canals, soon eclipsed the glory and majesty of the former capital, Ayutthaya. Rama I brought the country's

ROYAL PALACE
Thailand, Bangkok,
1782–1884

most talented architects to Bangkok and, on the only plateau in the city that is safe from flooding, laid the cornerstone for that legendary palace ensemble celebrated today as the crowning glory of Thai architecture.

The first building to rise within the over 200,000-square-meter area was the Temple of the Emerald Buddha (Wat Phra Kaeo), a sort of national shrine. The seventy-centimeter-high Buddha statue revered here is said to possess magical powers and to be a guardian of the country, a guarantor of independence, liberty, and prosperity throughout the empire. Since the days of Rama I it has been common practice for reigning kings to reclad the Buddha statue in a ritual held at the start of every new season. During the hot summer months the sculpture of the "Enlightened One" wears a golden tunic set with diamonds, during the monsoon period a blue garment shot through with golden threads, and in the cooler season, a cloak of pure gold.

Yet besides religion, science was at home in the new palace city. The Temple of the Reclining Buddha (Wat Pho), built in the sixteenth century and expanded by Rama I, was always a center of medicine, astronomy, and literature. In fact, all the rulers from the dynasty of Rama I have distinguished themselves to this day by learning, liberal thinking, and receptiveness to new developments. Rama II made a name for himself as a poet, Rama III brought American missionaries into the country, Rama IV was an expert on European history, and Rama V employed Danish engineers to build an electric streetcar line in Bangkok—ten years before the first streetcar rolled through Copenhagen.

2

3

4

Another European-inspired plan of Rama v's, however, failed. The enormous new Italian Renaissance-style residence (Chakri Maha Prasat) he built for his family from 1875 onwards met with resistance on the part of his courtiers, who found it too "exotic." The critics were placated only when Rama v agreed to adorn the Florentine facade with Far Eastern pointed roofs complete with rearing *naga* serpents and three towers in the style of traditional Thai architecture.

1  Wat Phra Kaeo, detail of wall
2  The ornate rooftops of the Royal Palace
3  The Temple of the Emerald Buddha, Wat Phra Kaeo
4  The royal family lived in the palace only until 1946. Now it is used for official functions, banquets, and ceremonies

It was all the fault of Dr. Richard Russell. Around the middle of the eighteenth century this Brighton physician discovered the therapeutic effects of seawater: heated, mixed with milk, and imbibed in small sips, he maintained, it was an excellent remedy for hypochondria, melancholy, and colic—in short, for aches and pains of all sorts. Hardly had he published this insight, when half London rushed to take a saltwater cure at the coastal town eighty kilometers to the south, rapidly transforming Brighton into England's most fashionable spa.

In 1783, it even received a visit from the twenty-one-year-old crown prince, the later King George IV. Although physical ailments brought him to Brighton, George also envisaged amorous adventures of the kind

*The kitchen in the Eastern Pavilion leaves little to be desired. Everything that one needs to perfect the culinary arts is available here. Your correspondent is hardly exaggerating in his proclamation that those who want to see the most modern, most comfortable, and most practical kitchen in all of Britain, must come to Brighton!*

C. Wright, *The Brighton Ambulator*, 1818

THE ROYAL PAVILION
England, Brighton, 1787–1823
Architects: Henry Holland and John Nash

his doting parents prevented him from having in the capital. And his hopes were not in vain. George met the love of his life in Brighton, Maria Fitzherbert, whom he secretly wed. Yet, not only was Maria six years his elder, widowed, and of middle-class origin, but even worse— she was a Catholic. George, the future head of the Anglican Church, could not allow himself to be seen with her in London.

So he established his "inofficial" spouse, who in 1795 would be augmented by an "official" one in the person of Caroline of Brunswick, in a villa in Brighton, and erected a refuge of his own right across the street. Although originally it was to be just a country house, the project soon got out of hand.

When the Royal Pavilion was finished, it evoked an opulent oriental fairy-tale palace. The exterior was dominated by cupolas, minarets, and stone arabesques, and the interior was an exotic wonderworld, a splendiferous Far Eastern tent filled with carved banana leaves, bamboo furniture, and mahogany chinoiseries. East Asian art was indeed in vogue at the time, for England was then in the process of extending her sway over the Indian subcontinent. Nevertheless, George's edifice was considered capricious, mocked at as an "oriental souvenir box," and denounced as the "concoction of a crazy bigamist of royal blood."

Yet George proved immune to such criticism. Throughout his life he took special pride in the kitchen with its technical improvements, including pressure cookers, ventilation hoods, and an automatic grill. Being a passionate host and gourmet, George spent his frequent sojourns in Brighton largely at the banquet table—which soon left its mark on his girth. The press mocked that he had gone as much out of shape as the pumpkin domes of the Royal Pavilion. George merely replied that it was not as a spa patient that he had spent the majority of his days in Brighton.

1  The palace by night
2  *George IV as Prince Regent*, painting by Sir Thomas
   Lawrence, *c.* 1814
3  The Royal Pavilion: a kingdom of marble, bamboo,
   gold, and mahogany
4  The Great Kitchen, renovated according to John Nash's
   plans

4

# PALACE OF THE WINDS   Jaipur

PALACE OF THE WINDS
India, Jaipur, 1799
Commissioned by: Maharaja
Pratap Singh

"One is tempted to believe that these facades and palaces had sprung from the exorbitant imagination of a poet," noted an Italian traveler in the 1920s after a visit to Jaipur. His words still hold true today. The capital of Rajasthan is one of the most magnificent and colorful cities in northern India—a fairy tale transformed into stone that is still celebrated in many travel reports as the quintessence of oriental exoticism. Not much has changed since the city was founded in the eighteenth century. Surrounded by a massive, crenellated wall, Jaipur evokes a stage set from *The Arabian Nights*.

Seat of a maharaja, or "great king," the palace zone encloses a panoply of stately pavilions, temples, courtyards, and gardens, constituting one of India's most splendid royal residences. The Palace of the Winds in the southeast part of the expansive grounds, whose popular name derives from its little weather vanes that respond to the slightest breeze, is perhaps the most original of all the architectural creations there. Yet its decorative facade is little more than a false front. Its bays and balconies conceal nothing more than galleries no wider than theater boxes, corridors, and stairways where ladies of the harem once jostled. They were forbidden to leave the palace and take part in public life. However, at least it provided the

maharaja's wives, concubines, and daughters with an opportunity to observe the hustle and bustle on the street without being seen themselves. The filigree sandstone lattice-work over the 953 windows shielded them from every inquisitive stare. Still, harem denizens likely took little pleasure in their compulsory isolation. According to a report from around 1700, they were permitted to "enjoy

the diversions of comedy and dance, hear fairy-tale and love stories, rest on blossom-strewn divans, stroll in the gardens, and listen to the murmuring of the rippling water." Otherwise, their lives were all monotony and boredom. But these times could not last. By 1875, as the India traveler Louis Rousselet reported, "In the absence of royal concubines and other beauties, the chambers of the harem are now populated only by noisy monkeys."

*In a harem, there usually reigns an atmosphere of lascivious sensuality, extravagant and dissolute festivity, overwhelming opulence, conspicuous refinement, and immeasurable vanity. The true ruler among the ladies, however, is intrigue.*

Francesco Pelsaert, *Writings Concerning Mogul India*, 1627

1  The Peacock gate in Jaipur's town palace
2  The rear facade of the Palace of the Winds
3  A fresco showing an Indian harem dancer
4  Arches, niches, bays, balconies, and filigree lattice-work windows carved out of sandstone
5  The Palace of the Winds is little more than a five-story facade

4

5

# A Princess' Elopement

# SULTAN'S PALACE   Zanzibar

OLD SULTAN'S PALACE
Tanzania, Zanzibar, 1828–34

When the broad-beamed freighters returned to their home port of Zanzibar, the sultan's children grew starry-eyed, because "the ships brought us all of our lovely play-things from Europe," as Princess Salme of Oman and Zanzibar (1844–1924) recalled in her memoirs. "Twenty to thirty boxes usually, filled to the top with little wagons, dolls, music boxes, harmonicas, flutes, and trumpets. If these things were not to our taste, the captain was in for trouble. After all, our father had given him only one order: Buy only the finest you can find, and shirk no expense." Money, indeed, was no object.

Zanzibar—capital of the island of the same name off the coast of East Africa—experienced an unprecedented heyday under Sultan Seyyid Said (1806–56), Princess Salme's father. In those days the lively harbor town was not only the point of departure for numerous expeditions that left for the heart of the "Black Continent" in search of the legendary sources of the Nile, but also the world's largest trading center for cloves, ivory—and slaves. It was an activity from which the sultan himself profited most. He made Zanzibar his official residence and added

*The ship made fast in the harbor. Immediately jewelry and silk dealers came on board, fruit vendors—and a magician in a red fez. He gave us a sample of his skills in the most wonderful gibberish. Behind him shone the blue sea, shimmered the white walls of Zanzibar, the Sultan's Palace flickered in the sunlight, and palms and melon trees rose into the azure sky. It was a marvelous sight, fabulous, colorful, and incandescent.*

Friedrich Schnack, *The Magician of Zanzibar*, 1951

an opulent palace to the picturesque cityscape, whose houses of shell and coral limestone, minarets, church steeples, and temples are now among the World Heritage sites of UNESCO.

Here resided Seyyid Said, doted on by 800 servants, in the midst of his 73 wives and 35 children. "The Sultan's Palace has a cheerful and friendly air," Princess Salme writes in her memoirs. "From every room one has a wonderful view of the sea and its ships—a picture that has engraved itself deep in my soul. And when darkness falls, the many colorful lanterns suspended from the ceiling make the whole house glow with a magical shimmer."

The economic boom on which all this luxury was based—including a portable lavatory with built-in water closet in the sultan's dressing room—attracted many foreigners to Zanzibar, then the most significant harbor city in East Africa. Branch offices of foreign trading companies rose on all hands. On one fateful day in 1866, it finally happened: Princess Salme fell in love with Heinrich Ruete, a young German merchant and representative of the Hamburg agency of Hansing & Co. Since the Koran forbade relationships between Muslim women and Christian men, and religious rules were strictly adhered to at the sultan's court, the couple had no choice but to elope.

Their first stop was Aden, where Princess Salme converted to Christianity, was baptized Emily, and married Heinrich. Then they proceeded to Hamburg. The princess' father-in-law was impressed by his son's conquest, and conceded that "the daughter of the Sultan of Zanzibar" was, "contrary to my expectations, a good housewife and as loveable a daughter-in-law as ever I could wish." Salme gave birth to three children—Antonie, Rudolph, and Rosalie—before her happiness crumbled, in 1870. Her husband died under the wheels of a horse-drawn trolley, and her ardent desire to return to Zanzibar remained unfulfilled, for her family had dispossessed her. "My tears are unquenchable," Salme wrote. "One after another rolls down my cheeks, like the waves of the sea." When she passed away in the German city of Jena in 1924, among Salme's few possessions was a bottle filled with Zanzibar sand.

1  Princess Salme of Oman and Zanzibar, later known as Emily Ruete
2  An engraving of Zanzibar, seen here from the Indian Ocean
3  Until 1964 all of Zanzibar's sultans resided in the so-called People's Palace
4  The Sultan's Palace is also known as the House of Wonders. On the left is the old palace, flanking the new one on the right

## *Castor and Pollux on the Main River*

# POMPEIANUM  Aschaffenburg

1

POMPEIANUM
Germany, Aschaffenburg,
1840–48
Architects: Friedrich von Gärt-
ner and Friedrich Andreas
Klumpp

Where the Main River leaves its quiet valley, you suddenly have the sense of entering a virtually Mediterranean atmosphere. The ridges of the hills descend in great sweeps, the climate feels unusually mild, vineyards spread over the rocky terraces along the slopes. Then, unexpectedly, you come upon a Roman villa: "Rosebeds and agaves, an atrium with columns, over which vaults a stretch of blue sky; in the walls the luminous red and warm ocher of Italy. This is perhaps the most remarkable architectural dream of King Ludwig 1 of Bavaria (1786 –1869) which has come true here," wrote a travel writer in the nineteenth century.

The monarch called his villa the "Pompeianum." Its model, the Casa di Castore e Polluce, in fact stands in Pompeii—that flourishing provincial town on the Gulf of Naples that suffocated under a heavy shroud of ash, dust, and incandescent lava when Mount Vesuvius erupted on August 24 of A.D. 79. When the buried city was rediscovered by treasure hunters seventeen centuries later, the scholarly world was beside itself with amazement.

Bulwer-Lytton's novel *The Last Days of Pompeii* appeared, the enthusiasm of the King of Bavaria, a great admirer of Greco-Roman antiquity, knew no bounds.

Ludwig 1 traveled to the Gulf of Naples to inspect the excavations, accompanied by his architect, Friedrich von Gärtner. He sketched the ruins and collected the ground plan of a house, discovered in 1828, where the archaeologists had found a mural depicting Castor and Pollux, the sons of Zeus. So taken by the Casa di Castore e Polluce was the king that he decided to build a replica of it back home—in Aschaffenburg. The local populace was engrossed in the king's exotic project. They collected at the building site in such great numbers that Ludwig, fearing construction delays, forbid entry on pain of punishment. When the work was done, the two interior courts were encompassed by a range of premises with Latin names—including a tablinum (reception room), an aerarium (treasury), a culina (kitchen), two triclinia (dining rooms), several cubicula (bedrooms), and a whole series of cellae (chambers) for slaves. An elaborate mosaic with the words "Cave Canum" cautioned against the vicious dog.

However, Ludwig 1 kept neither a dog, let alone slaves, at his Pompeianum. He did not even live there. At no time was the villa conceived as a royal refuge. It was intended solely as a monument to ancient civilization— an object lesson for art lovers and an enterable model of a noble Roman residence, on a 1:1 scale. Even the garden, the king desired, was to be suffused with a Mediterranean mood. Yet as the northern climate refused to play along, certain subterfuges were resorted to. The envisaged cypresses were replaced by plain trees, the umbrella pines by black spruces. The grapevines below the villa, on the other hand, flourished wonderfully, and a considerable yield of wine is still bottled from them every year.

*In the Pompeian house one feels spirited back into the ancient world. It has turned out superbly, I am delighted. The murals are wonderfully successful as well. Come to Germany, then you will see the Pompeianum with its orange trees, its cypresses, and all the other Southern plants.*

King Ludwig I of Bavaria, writing to Martin von Wagner, his art agent in Rome, 1851

1  Pompeian house in Aschaffenburg, illustration by Friedrich von Gärtner
2  The southern facade of the Pompeianum with Johannisburg Palace in the background
3  The re-created back wall of the pleasure gardens
4  The atrium

Nowhere else had everyday utensils, works of art, and paintings from the Roman era been more perfectly preserved than under the stone-hard volcanic mass in Pompeii. Publications with illustrations of the treasures brought to light became bestsellers. When Edward

4 >

2                    3

Archduke Maximilian of Austria (1832–67) loved the sea, its infinite expanse as well as its ever-changing aspects. On one afternoon though, it almost spelled his end. In 1855, as he was sailing in his small yacht *Madonna della Salute*, the sky suddenly darkened and a violent squall arose. Only at the last moment was the boat able to reach the safe harbor of Grignano. The storm was so strong that it forced the sailing party to spend the night in a fisherman's cottage. The next morning, the sun shone from a clear sky as if nothing had happened—and Maximilian felt himself spirited into a Garden of Eden. The lovely countryside around his safe haven and the breathtaking views along the coast towards Trieste so charmed the

*Very close to the sea on the Punta Grignana, perched on a precipitous promontory like an eagle's nest, rises the Castle of Miramare. Here the young Archduke Maximilian dreamed his finest dreams, here he could indulge his poetic enthusiasms. And when he let his gaze roam, the entire glory of the Adriatic lay unfolded before him, with its swelling sails, its brilliant blue, and the far shores in the hazy mist.*

Tuisco Achilles Liegel, *Emperor Maximilian of Mexico: Recollections from the Life of an Unfortunate Ruler*, 1868

twenty-three-year-old that he knew that he must settle here.

So he had a residence erected: Miramare, from whose windows, balconies, and terraces Maximilian could continually "admire the sea." By Christmas Eve 1860, construction had progressed to the point that he and his wife, Carlota, were able to move into their private apartments on the ground floor. Some of the rooms had been furnished in the style of ships' cabins by the young archduke, who since 1854 had been commander-in-chief of the Austrian navy. His study, for instance, was based on the admiral's cabin on the *Novara*, flagship of the imperial fleet, where he conferred with his staff. Maximilian's love of the sea also showed in the Seagull Hall with its delightful renderings of seagulls on the ceiling, in salons with wall coverings of sky-blue damask adorned with miniature anchors, and in the Compass Hall, which featured a

**MIRAMARE CASTLE**
Italy, near Trieste, 1856–70
Architect: Carl Junker

compass on the ceiling that was connected with a weathervane on deck, hereby indicated the prevailing wind direction.

For the luxuriant gardens that were wrested from the rocky soil behind the castle, Maximilian brought exotic plants and trees back with him from a journey to Brazil. Visitors often came upon him here, amid oleanders and olive trees, standing before his easel, capturing on canvas the play of light and color. Such occupations, however, found an abrupt end when, at the behest of Napoleon III, Maximilian was chosen to become emperor of Mexico. Barely thirty-two at the time, he long hesitated before accepting. But then, on April 10, 1864, in the presence of a Mexican delegation at Miramare Castle, Maximilian took the oath of office as the flag of his future empire was raised above the castle tower. Four days later a state bark brought him from the castle's harbor to the frigate *Novara* anchored in the bay, and his Atlantic crossing began.

It was to be a journey of no return. Maximilian's brief reign in Mexico proved hapless. Caught between rival political factions, he was condemned to death, and on June 19, 1867, two and a half weeks before his thirty-fifth birthday, Maximilian was executed by a firing squad. Only the coffin with his body returned to Europe on the *Novara*, his beloved ship. But people were aware of the honor they owed him. After the frigate had anchored off Trieste and Maximilian's remains had been transferred to the Austrian royal hearse, the mourning procession first stopped at nearby Miramare Castle before continuing on to Vienna and the Capuchin Mausoleum.

1  The castle in a drawing by Albert Rieger, 1865
2  Seagull Hall in a photograph from the archduke's personal album
3  The castle was built of striking white limestone, making it visible from the city of Trieste in the distance
4  Edouard Manet, *Execution of the Emperor Maximilian*, 1867
5  The castle's interior has been preserved in its original state

3

4

5

No one would maintain that Ludwig II (1845–86) suffered under a housing shortage. The fairy-tale king always had luxuriously furnished apartments at his disposal: at the Munich and Würzburg residences, the Imperial Castle at Nuremberg, and Trausnitz Castle in Landshut. On a whim he could establish his court at his castles on Lake Starnberg or in Algäu. Rooms were also reserved and furnished for him at various idyllically located country inns. There were also the twelve extremely comfortable hunting seats he had inherited from his father. Still, he was dissatisfied.

Ever since he had found a box of building blocks under the Christmas tree at age seven and began stacking them into houses, castles, and churches, building had been Ludwig II's consuming passion. He was a passionate imi-

*Shades of a new plan: a chivalric castle in the Old German, Romantic style. In the main building my apartments (Gothic, richly carved, paneled), banquet hall, guest rooms, projecting bays, chapel (ceiling blue with stars, medieval glass windows). In the tower, adjutant's quarters, spiral staircase as far up as it can go.*

King Ludwig II of Bavaria, diary entry of April 16, 1868

NEUSCHWANSTEIN CASTLE
Germany, near Füssen,
1869–92
Design: Christian Jank
Architects: Eduard von Riedel, Georg Dollmann, and Julius Hofmann

tator of other people's architecture. He built an enormous conservatory based on London's Crystal Palace on the roof of the Munich Residence, erected a miniature palace à la Madame de Pompadour's Petit Trianon in Oberammergau, and established a second Versailles on an island in Lake Chiem. Then, high in the Bavarian Alps, Ludwig built a Swiss chalet complete with a "Moorish Hall." There, clad in oriental garb, he used to celebrate his birthdays, "while his servants, costumed as Muslims, lolled around on carpets and cushions, immersed in the vapors of incense, smoking hookahs and sipping mocha," as the wife of a court official later recalled.

The most frequently visited of Ludwig's monuments to himself is doubtless Neuschwanstein, his "Castle of the Grail," near Füssen in the province of Algäu. "I am very much looking forward to dwelling there," he wrote to the composer Richard Wagner shortly after construction work began. "You enjoy a wonderful view of the Tyrolean Mountains and far across the plain. The spot is one of the loveliest that can be found, sacred and inapproachable, a worthy temple for you, my divine friend."

Ludwig had the interiors furnished in medieval style and decorated with scenes from Germanic legends. Still, he did not wish to dispense with the achievements of modern technology—toilets with automatic flushes, an electric intercom system, and even a telephone were installed. In 1869, Ludwig admitted that as a monarch he faced "nothing but bothers the livelong day," so he simply had to create such paradises "where no earthly burden shall reach me." This latter wish, however, was destined to be in vain. At Neuschwanstein, of all places, the fate of the fairy-tale King began to run its irrevocable course.

There, on the night of June 12, 1886, Ludwig was arrested, placed under the control of a trustee, and declared deposed. Without making any effort whatsoever at diagnosis, four mental specialists had reached the conclusion that Ludwig was insane. The best proof of that, they said, was Neuschwanstein Castle itself. Barely forty-eight hours later, the king was dead. By his own hand, if the official reports are to be believed.

5 >

1 View of the castle in winter
2 Washbasin in Ludwig II's bedroom
3 King Ludwig II in a photograph by Joseph Albert
4 The throne room
5 Neuschwanstein—the fairy-tale king's dream that became reality

# A Haven of Peace

# ACHILLEION    Corfu

To the Greeks, she was simply "the train." This was not meant disrespectfully. On the contrary, they marvelled at the incredible pace with which the agile lady walked the island of Corfu, in every direction. But her haste had a deeper reason: throughout her life, Empress Elizabeth of Austria (1837–98), the famous "Sisi," was on the escape. Etiquette at the Viennese court, her obligations, her mother-in-law, and her husband, poisoned her life. So she kept forever on the move, seldom even spending the Christmas holidays at home with her family—prompting a newspaper to remark sarcastically that Elizabeth was "the most charming guest at the Vienna Hofburg." Nor was Emperor Francis Joseph overly astonished when his wife, prone as she was to "nervous crises," announced after thirty-four years of marriage that she looked upon Greece as her "future home."

On many journeys she had long since become familiar with the country and its people, its history and mythology, and she spoke modern Greek as fluently as French, English, and Hungarian. Corfu held a special appeal for her, ever since a stay there for health reasons in summer 1861. Elizabeth thought this northernmost of the Ionian islands the "loveliest point in the world." It gave her something after which she had sought in vain in Vienna: peace of mind. So about ten kilometers south of the capital, on a hill by the sea with a view of the Albanian moun-

1

*Here in this home, which she built herself from the ground up and where she wished to be only herself, the lines of her exalted soul appeared all the more clearly: singing sadnesses, colors without a name, nuances like expiring fragrances, darkened golds from forgotten eras.*

Diary entry of Constantin Christomanos,
describing Empress Elizabeth and her Achilleion, 1899

2

ACHILLEION
Greece, Corfu, 1888–92
Architect: Raffaele Carito

tains, Elizabeth had a palace built in the Pompeian style. The snow-white building was invisible from the interior of the island and complete, in Elizabeth's day, with its own landing-stage. She dedicated it to her favorite Greek hero, Achilles, "because for me he personifies the Greek soul and the beauty of the landscape and the people." She also felt him to be a kindred spirit: "He was strong and obstinate, despised all traditions, held only his own will sacred, and lived out his own dreams alone."

Elizabeth set out to do the same. She viewed Corfu as an "asylum where I can belong entirely to myself." Reading in the works of Heinrich Heine until late at night, she used to spend the early morning hours composing poetry

in the colonnade. "She is the loneliest of the lonely," noted Constantin Christomanos in his diary, the young man she hired to read to her. Yet, this is exactly what she wished to be. Coming upon her otherwise so valued companion in the garden at five o'clock one morning, she sent Christomanos away, furious "as a dark angel who had an Eden to defend."

1    Temple dedicated to Heinrich Heine, the Empress' favorite
     poet
2    The castle's colonnade and garden of the muses
3,4  The palace and terrace with a view of the sea

3

4

# MONTAZAH PALACE Alexandria

1

MONTAZAH PALACE
Egypt, Alexandria, 1892–1932
Architects: Antonio Lasciac
and Ernesto Verrucci

It was the same as every year when the Egyptian summer began: whoever could afford it fled from the searing heat in the interior to the Mediterranean coast. Nor could the thirty-two-year-old King Farouk I (1920–65; reigned 1936–52) bear to stay in sultry Cairo. In early June he gave the signal to start. A packed convoy of dark limousines got underway, ferrying him and his retinue to Alexandria. The "Pearl of the Mediterranean," as the venerable metropolis on the western tip of the Nile Delta was known, had been a favorite summering spot of Egyptian rulers since antiquity. Cleopatra had spent the hottest months in a palace that lay right on the waterside. From her apartments she could gaze upon the renowned lighthouse of Alexandria, one of the Seven Wonders of the World. And anchored in the harbor was her ship of state, whose sails were reputedly doused in perfume. Admittedly, the glory of ancient days soon paled.

But in the nineteenth century Alexandria experienced a second heyday. The city became a mecca for European travelers, émigrés, and bohemians, a cosmopolitan oasis that attracted aristocrats, artists, writers, and intellectuals who thirsted for insights into the land of the pharaohs with its pyramids, temples, and legendary Valley of the

> *The public gardens lie to the south of the summer residence, scene of the famous court balls of Alexandria. The various approaches to this park are packed with elegant carriages, especially on Thursdays and Sundays. Here the big city revels unashamedly in luxury. And in the afternoon, a military band plays European and Arabian symphonies.*
>
> François Levernay, *Alexandria. Guide and Yearbook for Egypt*, 1892

Kings. A flourishing trade in cotton and the opening of the Suez Canal in 1869 did the rest—Alexandria became a world city once again, whose coffeehouses and boulevards were the most fashionable in all of North Africa. Not only foreigners came in droves. Prosperous Egyptians, too, fell under the spell of Alexandria's charm, and appreciated its cool, continually refreshing breezes. Soon the entire coastline was dotted with stately villas.

The culmination of that building boom was Montazah Palace, at the eastern edge of the city. The summer residence of the Egyptian ruling dynasty stood on Gazelle Hill, a cliff overlooking the sea. It is a fabulous site, with a breathtaking view over the Mediterranean to the north and encompassed on the south, east, and west by an enchanting garden of palms and pines roamed by

gazelles, an idyllic bay, and a high wall that shields the noble refuge from the noise of the coastal road. The cornerstone was laid by Abbas II Hilmi (1874–1944; reigned 1892–14), who had attended boarding schools in Switzerland and Austria. It was he who built the Salamlek—a daunting edifice based on the City Palace of Vienna.

King Fuad I (1868–1936; reigned 1917–36) was more an *aficionado* of Italy. He commissioned the "Haramlek," a fairy-tale castle on the 114-acre grounds whose loggia-dotted facade recalls a Florentine palazzo and whose soaring tower resembles the Torre del Mangia, the tower of the city hall of Siena, in Tuscany. The final contractor, whose additions were rather modest by comparison, was King Farouk I. With him the tradition of the Montazah Palace as a summer residence of the Egyptian ruling dynasty came to an end. A corrupt and hated monarch, Farouk was at breakfast at the Haramlek on July 24, 1952, when he learned of his dethronement, which would be followed a year later by the declaration of a republic. Initially Farouk hoped to be able to delay things. Clad in a red dressing gown, he rushed to the telephone, to try to prevent the unstoppable. Flight remained his only option. He was never to see Montazah Palace again. Farouk died, an exile in Rome, in 1965.

1 King Farouk I of Egypt with British forces during World War II
2 Montazah Palace was built to be the summer residence
3 The light tower of Alexandria was said to be one of the Seven Wonders of the World
4 The palace and lighthouse in the bay of Montazah

2

3

4

# BAHIA PALACE Marrakech

BAHIA PALACE
Morocco, Marrakech,
1894–1900
Architect: Muhammad
al-Mekki

Everything was supposed to be much smaller and simpler, but the project gradually slipped out of the architect's control. It was all the fault of Si Moussa, the contractor, a former slave. Advanced to the position of grand vizier to Sultan Abd al-Rahman (reigned 1822–59), and as such prime minister of the Sultanate of Marrakech, Si Moussa literally went overboard. As construction work proceeded, he bought lot after lot and ordered annex after annex to his future residence. The original plans had to be revised continually. This not only confused his architects but also ultimately baffled Si Moussa himself. When the builders and artists had left, the palace spread out as a twenty-acre, sprawling labyrinth of interlocking courtyards, corridors, chambers, halls, and stairwells.

*Silently Bahia Palace awaits the waking hour. Exhausted and weary, the night still lingers in the perfumed branches. The sultan's grand vizier, around whose nocturnal favors the hopes of the harem revolved, could now retire to his chambers, much in need of rest. But before he was overcome by sleep, perhaps he thought about the costs of the building and the endless time it took to erect it.*

From the documentary film *Marrakech: Pearl of the South*, by Josef Becker

But it certainly suited Marrakech. In its picturesque confusion, the palace appears just as unmethodical as the tangle of the bazaars, the countless colorful markets that still represent the source of Marrakech's prosperity today. As Elias Canetti, Nobel Prize winner for literature, noted, "there is a bazaar for spices and one for leather goods. The rope makers have their place, as do the basket makers and jewelers. Among the carpet vendors,

some have large, spacious vaults, and hardly do you think that 'today I wouldn't mind some dyed yarn,' you see it hanging in broad swaths to your left and right, in purple, in dark blue, in sunny yellow and black."

Trade has flourished in the old sultans' city for centuries, and it was with the merchants that everything once began. Marrakech was first known as a crossroads of caravan routes. Here goats' skins from the south were bartered for cedar wood from the north, dried fish from the west for red pepper from the east. Nevertheless, the bustling trade center with its magnificent backdrop of snowcapped Atlas Mountains was reputedly a dismal place back then. Its lush palm groves, legend has it, did not grow until nomads besieged Marrakech and nonchalantly spit out the pits of their date ration.

At any rate, the city burgeoned into a flowering oasis, and was soon considered the loveliest in the land. It was "the pearls of the south, cast over the High Atlas," as an Arabian poet wrote. No wonder the country's rulers settled within its walls. Even the name of the country derives from that of the city—"Morocco" is a distortion of "Marrakech," and goes back to seventeenth-century European merchants. The natives had no objection to the name, as long as the foreigners continued to bring goods and money to the city. One of those who profited was Si Moussa.

His labyrinthine palace, unimpressive from the outside and named after his favorite wife, unfolds in *Arabian Nights* glory inside: the floors paved with multicolored marble, the walls covered with painted tiles, the columns decorated with glass mosaics. From the ceilings hang exquisite chandeliers and the furniture is of the finest cedar—all in a setting of superb Moorish stuccowork. In 1961 the palace went down in cinema history, when scenes for *Lawrence of Arabia* were filmed there.

The Moroccans still talk about it for other reasons though. The palace took seven years to build, much longer than originally planned. This is why even today, when a matter has finally been settled after lengthy, enervating debate, one often hears people exclaim, "At last, Bahia is finished!"

1

2

3

4

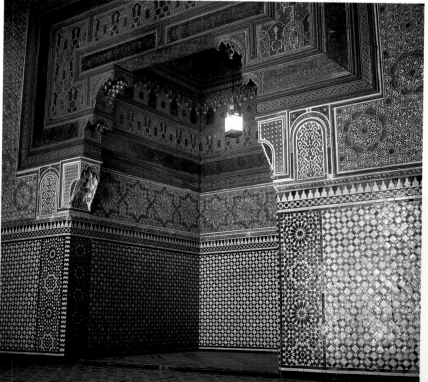

1 The palace's courtyard
2 Moresque gardens and fountains adorning the
   courtyard
3 Bahia Palace is also know as the
   "glittering palace"
4 The remarkable mosaic wall

# PRESIDENT'S PALACE Havana

PRESIDENT'S PALACE
Cuba, Havana, 1913–20

On October 10, 1940, low clouds hung over Havana, and it was raining cats and dogs. In spite of the downpour, tens of thousands of people had gathered to celebrate the election victory of General Fulgencio Batista Zaldívar (1901–73). He had fought his way up through the ranks from petty bourgeois origins, and was now the new president of Cuba. At twelve o'clock sharp Batista stepped out onto the balcony of the President's Palace, "an umbrella over his head," as the Cuban author Miguel Barnet recalled. "But before he began to speak, he waved the umbrella carrier aside, and braved the rain unprotected. The crowd clapped and howled until they were hoarse. The army music corps played the national anthem, and in front of the palace, police patrol cars circled, their sirens making a deafening noise."

All of Cuba's hopes rested on Batista. Its inhabitants dreamed of a revival of the good mood that prevailed in

*In the neo-Baroque festival hall of the former President's Palace, a video projector from the ex-German Democratic Republic was showing a propaganda film on the Cuban army that automatically started over and over again. The sole audience, an unarmed female soldier in a green uniform, slept soundly on one of the uncomfortable chairs. This is the room where guests of state used to be received, I was told by a guard.*

Alfred Herzka, *Cuba—Farewell to the Commandante?* 1998

the years from 1900 to 1920. Back then, the prices for sugar cane—the country's principal export—had climbed to such astronomical heights that everyone was talking of a "dance of millions." The growing prosperity of those times showed itself most clearly in Havana. Within the space of a few years, the fabled "Queen of the Carribean," was transformed into a brilliant, European-style metropolis. Stately company headquarters shot up, elegant townhouses, luxurious shopping streets, and exclusive first-class hotels. Even the government entered the architectural competition. It commissioned the monumental President's Palace, and had it furnished by Tiffany's Glass and Decorating Company, New York.

Yet the presidents who resided in these exquisite surroundings from 1920 onwards were, with few exceptions, corrupt tyrants who had come to power through the fixing of elections, or coups. Personal enrichment, nepotism, and abuse of power were the order of the day. The rulers concerned themselves little with the worries of the common people. When sugar prices fell through the floor, poverty spread and social unrest began to break out, they knew no better than to react dictatorially. Cuba's economy had since fallen largely into the hands of American corporations that were ruthlessly skimming off profits. Batista, everyone thought, would turn things around and bring back the good times.

Yet they were mistaken. The well-nigh omnipotent master of the "Sugar Island" reacted no differently than his hated predecessors. Corruption burgeoned to an unprecedented scale, the state-condoned trade in alcohol and drugs, gambling and prostitution, flourished. Cuba became the "backyard and bordello of the U.S.A." At the same time, Batista's secret police pursued critics of the regime with increasing brutality, even stringing up their mutilated bodies on street lamps as a warning to others.

At carnival time in 1953, a young attorney by the name of Fidel Castro and about 100 supporters staged a revolt. Their attempt to storm a barracks was just as abortive as an attack, four years later, on the President's Palace. Their aim, to capture and execute Batista, had failed. Not until 1958, five years after the first attempt, would their fortunes change. Castro, now supported by Ernesto "Che" Guevara and commander of a rebel army of about 50,000 men, managed to defeat Batista's troops. The dictator was deeply shaken. But he put up a good face, even holding a rousing New Year's Eve party at the President's Palace, long after having packed his suitcases.

On January 1, 1959, at two in the morning, Batista fled the country for the Dominican Republic, taking along with him the golden TV from the festival hall and 35 million dollars from the state coffers. Just a few weeks later, the Museum of the Revolution was opened in his former residence. Its treasures include none of the valuable Tiffany objects, only the guerillas' empty Kalashnikovs, worn leather boots, and blood-caked trousers.

1 The former President's Palace now houses the Museum of the Revolution
2 Fidel Castro giving one of his legendary speeches in Santiago de Cuba, 1964
3 Havana in Batista's time
4 Inside the museum

1

4

2

3

## An American Dream

# HEARST CASTLE San Simeon

HEARST CASTLE
U.S.A., San Simeon,
California, 1919–47
Architect: Julia Morgan

Julia Morgan, the first female architecture graduate of the Académie des Beaux-Arts in Paris, wondered what was in store for her. She had received a telephone call from the American media mogul William Randolph Hearst (1863–1951), who asked whether she might not like to accompany him on a jaunt to San Simeon, on the Pacific coast. There he would show her all the antiques that were in such urgent need of adequate housing. Julia Morgan naturally agreed, and when she got there, she could hardly believe what she saw.

The barns scattered over the huge Hearst family estate, originally intended for agricultural equipment, were close to bursting with works of art. Under a thick layer of dust and cobwebs, Roman amphoras, statues of gods, Gothic traveling trunks, chimneypieces, saints' figures, Flemish tapestries, and Old Master paintings stood in expectation of better days. In one of the barns, Hearst had mothballed the separate pieces of a massive coffered ceiling from an Italian palazzo, in another, box upon box

*Far from the bustle of the cities the breeze sweeps over rolling green hills. The pines sigh softly, the ocean sparkles below. In this charming setting, the publisher William Randolph Hearst has erected a castle that looks like a Spanish cathedral. The three guesthouses resemble French villas, and the swimming pool is framed by an antique temple facade, as well as colonnades in the Greek style. It is all so unreal that you think you're dreaming.*

Based on Oliver Carlson and Ernest Sutherland Bates, Hearst: *Lord of San Simeon*, 1936

of silver table services—and a massive wrought-iron grate from a Spanish monastery.

The billionaire American publisher, who at the apex of his career owned twenty-six newspapers, thirteen periodicals, eight radio stations, and his own press service, was veritably obsessed with art. But he was also a knowledge-able connoisseur. As an assistant recalled, catalogues of the great auction houses were Hearst's daily reading, and when he was in Europe, he rushed from one auction. You could hold any sculpture under his nose, said his assistant, and he knew immediately where it was from, of what era, and from which school. He erred as seldom as any antique dealer in Paris or London.

Yet the media czar not only wanted to possess treasures but to display them, and for that he needed Julia Morgan. She was to create a setting for his works of art into which, for instance, the carved wood choir stalls Hearst had imported from France would fit to a tee. Thus began the story of the tycoon's "fabulous edifice" on his family property high above the Pacific coast. Many a stringent art lover might bristle at the sight of this supposed "castle." Yet regardless of the debate whether it represents an artistic misunderstanding worthy of a Hollywood producer, Hearst Castle is definitely unique. Nowhere else has eclecticism reached such dizzying heights.

Charlie Chaplin, Charles Lindbergh, Winston Churchill, and George Bernard Shaw strolled, as Hearst's guests, over Roman mosaics and Moorish tiles, spent nights in rooms furnished with exquisite period pieces, and refreshed themselves in the fabulous pool. Then again, to save money, Hearst installed coin telephones for his otherwise pampered guests, and wherever a Gobelin was to be hung in front of a wall, he decided that plastering was unnecessary. It is at these spots that the true building material of Hearst Castle reveals itself—reinforced concrete.

1 The main part of the Spanish-style building is the Casa Grande
2 The indoor Roman Pool
3 William Rudolph Hearst and Julia Morgan, the castle's architect
4 Unique aspects of the Neptune Pool include the oil-burning heating system, the Vermont marble decorating the pools and colonnades, and four 17th-century Italian bas-reliefs on the sides

# SUGGESTED READING

**Windsor Castle, Windsor**   page 12

De-la-Noy, Michael, *Windsor Castle. Past and Present*, London 1990
Farrar, Henry, *Windsor: Town and Castle*, London 2001
Hugh, Robert, *For the King's Pleasure*, Chichester 1990
Robinson, John M., *Windsor Castle. A Short History*, London 1996


**Prague Castle, Prague**   page 14

Burian, Jirí, *Prague Castle*, Prague 1989
Charles Prince of Schwarzenberg (Ed.), et al., *Prague Castle and its Treasures*,
   New York 1994
Fucíková, Eliska (Ed.), *Rudolf II and Prague: the Court and the City*, London 1997


**The Louvre, Paris**   page 16

Daufresne, Jean-Claude, *Le Louvre et les Tuileries*, Paris 1994
Farcy, Elisabeth de, and Frédéric Morvan, *Louvre*, Cologne 1995
Faÿ, Bernard, *Louis XVI; or the End of a World*, Chicago 1968
Hardman, John, *Louis XVI*, London 2000
Mitterrand, François, *The Grand Louvre: History of a Project*, New York, 1993
Pei, Ieoh M., Emile Biasini, and Jean Lacouture, *The Grand Louvre: A Museum
   Transfigured 1981–1993*, New York 1989


**The Hofburg, Vienna**   page 18

Eigl, Kurt, *Imperial Castle*, Vienna 1978
Herre, Franz, *Wien. Historische Spaziergänge*, Cologne 1992
Neumann, Paul, *A Guide to the Hofburg*, Vienna 1969


**Chateâu of Blois, Blois**   page 20

Balzac, Honoré de, *The Human Comedy*, 1842
Lesueur, Frédéric, *Le Château de Blois*, Paris 1970
Mahoney, Irene, *Madame Catherine*, New York 1975


**The Alhambra, Granada**   page 22

Grabar, Oleg, *The Alhambra*, London 1978
Irving, Washington, *The Alhambra*, adapted by Josephine V. Brown,
   Boston 1917
Stierlin, Henri and Anne, *Alhambra*, Paris 1991


**Doge's Palace, Venice**   page 24

Franzoi, Umberto, *The Doge's Palace in Venice*, Venice 1973
Franzoi, Umberto, Terisio Pignatti, and Wolfgang Wolters, *Il Palazzo Ducale di
   Venezia*, Treviso 1990
Honour, Hugh, *The Companion Guide to Venice*, Woodbridge 1997


**Imperial Palace, Beijing**   page 26

Aisin-Gioro, Pu Yi, *From Emperor to Citizen: the Autobiography of Aisin-Gioro Pu Yi*,
   Beijing 1989
MacFarquhar, Roderick, et al., *The Forbidden City*, New York 1972
Wan-go Wenig and Yang Boda, *The Palace Museum, Peking: Treasures of the For-
   bidden City*, New York 1982


**City Palace, Berlin**   page 28

Peschken, Goerd and Hans-Werner Klünner, *Das Berliner Schloß*, Frankfurt am
   Main/Berlin 1991
Rollka, Bodo and Klaus-Dieter Wille, *Das Berliner Stadtschloß. Geschichte und
   Zerstörung*, postscript by Wolf Jobst Siedler, Berlin 1993


**Vatican Palace, Rome**   page 30

Bergman, Robert P., *Vatican Treasures*, Cleveland 1998
Cloulas, Ivan, *The Borgias*, New York 1989
Fagiolo dell'Arco, Maurizio (Ed.), *Art of the Popes: From the Vatican Collection:
   How Pontiffs, Architects, Painters, and Sculptors Created the Vatican*, New York 1983
Giudici, Vittorio, *The Sistine Chapel*, New York 2000
Morello, Giovanni (Ed.), *2000 Years of Art and Culture in the Vatican and Italy*,
   Milan/New York 1993


**Palazzo Pitti, Florence**   page 32

Chiarini, Marco and Elisa Acanfora, *Pitti Palace: All the Museums, All the Works:
   The Official Guide*, Livorno 2001
Cleugh, James, *Medici: A Tale of Fifteen Generations*, New York 1975
Gurrieri, Francesco and Patrizia Fabbri, *Palaces of Florence*, New York 1996


**Topkapı Palace, Istanbul**   page 34

Davis, Fanny, *The Palace of Topkapi in Istanbul*, New York 1970
Goodwin, Godfrey, *Topkapi Palace*, London 1999
Hellier, Chris and Francesco Venuti, *Splendors of Istanbul: Houses and Palaces
   Along the Bosporus*, New York 1993


**Terem Palace, Moscow**   page 36

Ascher, Abraham, *The Kremlin*, New York 1972
Douglas Duncan, David, *Great Treasures of the Kremlin*, New York 1968
Vyuyeva, Natalia and Anastasia Pavlova, *The Grand Kremlin Palace*, Moscow
   1995


**Holyroodhouse, Edinburgh**   page 38

Bold, Alan, *Holyroodhouse*, London 1980
Montgomery-Massingberd, Hugh, *Great Houses of Scotland*, New York 1997
Smith Richardson, James, *The Abbey and Palace of Holyroodhouse*, Edinburgh 1978

**Hampton Court, London**   page 40

Baumann, Uwe, *Henry VIII in History, Historiography, and Literature*, New York 1991
Fraser, Antonia, *The Six Wives of Henry VIII*, London 1992
Nash, Roy, *Hampton Court. The Palace and the People*, London 1983


**Chateâu of Chambord, Loire Valley**   page 42

Chatenet, Monique, *Chambord*, Paris 2001
Tanguy, Geneviève-Morgane, *Mille et une Nuits de Chambord*, Chambray 1998
Trézin, Christian, *Chambord*, Rennes 1992
Vigny, Alfred de, *Cinq-Mars: or, A Conspiracy under Louis XIII*, 1826


**Noordeinde Palace, The Hague**   page 44

Aafjes, Bertus, *Haag*, The Hague 1955
Boer, Paul den, *Het Hùijts int Noordeynde. The Royal Palace Noordeinde in an Historical View*, Zutphen 1986
Haasse, Hella S. and S. W. Jackma, *A Stranger in the Hague: The Letters of Queen Sophie of the Netherlands to Lady Maler, 1842–1877*, Durham 1989


**Fontainebleau Palace, Fontainebleau**   page 46

Champigneulle, Bernard, *Versailles and Fontainebleau*, Munich 1984
Gallo, Max, *Napoleon*, 2 Vols., Berlin 2002
Lamartine, Alphonse de, *History of the Restoration*, 1815


**Gripsholm Castle, near Mariefried**   page 48

Bemmann, Helga, *Kurt Tucholsky. Ein Lebensbild*, Berlin 1990
Hepp, Michael, *Kurt Tucholsky*, Hamburg 1998
Johnsson, Ulf G., *Gripsholm*, Stockholm 1990


**Alcázar, Toledo**   page 50

Alcocer, Pedro de, *Hystoria o Descripción dela imperial Cibdad de Toledo*, Reprint of the 1554 edition, Madrid 1973


**Heidelberg Castle, Heidelberg**   page 52

Garden, Donald S., *Heidelberg*, Carlton 1972
Godfrey, Elizabeth, *Heidelberg, its Princes and its Palaces*, London 1906
Kölmel, Karl, *Guide to Heidelberg Castle*, Heidelberg 1952


**El Escorial, near Madrid**   page 54

Hernández Ferrero, Juan A., *The Royal Palaces of Spain*, New York 1997
Mulcahy, Rosmarie, *The Decoration of the Royal Basilica of El Escorial*, New York 1994
Ruiz-Larrea Cangas, César, *El Escorial. La Arquitectura del Monasterio*, Madrid 1986


**Aranjuez Palace, Aranjuez**   page 56

Junquera de Vega, Paulina and Teresa Ruiz Alcon, *Palacio Real de Aranjuez*, Madrid 1985
Schiller, Friedrich, *Don Carlos. Infante of Spain, a Drama in Five Acts*, New York 1959
Wade, Graham, *Joaquín Rodrigo and the Concierto de Aranjuez*, Leeds 1985


**Imperial Palace, Tokyo**   page 58

Dunn, Charles and Laurence Broderick, *Everyday Life in Traditional Japan*, New York 1997
Kaempfer, Engelbert, *The History of Japan: Together with a Description of the Kingdom of Siam 1690–1692*, n.d.
Reischauer, Edwin Oldfather, *Japan. The Story of a Nation*, New York 1998


**Hellbrunn Palace, Salzburg**   page 60

Bigler, Robert R., *Schloß Hellbrunn. Wunderkammer der Gartenarchitektur*, Vienna 1996
Martin, Franz, *Schloß Hellbrunn bei Salzburg*, Vienna/Augsburg 1925
Woods, May, *Italian Water Jokes and Automata at Schloß Hellbrunn in Austria*, in *Follies. The International Magazine for Follies, Grottoes, and Garden Buildings*, Vol. 10, Nr. 4 (1999)


**Potala Palace, Lhasa**   page 62

Dalai Lama, *Freedom in Exile: the Autobiography of the Dalai Lama*, New York 1990
Guise, Anthony (Ed.), *The Potala of Tibet*, London 1988
Harrer, Heinrich, *Seven Years in Tibet*, Thorndike 1998


**Versailles Palace, Versailles**   page 64

Archimbaud, Nicholas d', *Versailles*, Munich 2001
Hoog, Simone and Béatrix Saule, *Versailles*, Versailles 2000
Lévêque, Jean-Jacques, *Versailles*, Courberoie 2000


**Drottningholm Castle, Lake Mälar**   page 66

Beijer, Agne, *Court Theatres of Drottningholm and Gripsholm*, New York 1972
Mårtenson, Jan and Gunnar Brusewitz, *Drottningholm. The Palace on the Lakeside*, Stockholm 1985


**Nymphenburg Palace, Munich**   page 68

Hager, Luisa, *Nympenburg Palace, Park, Pavilions*, Munich 1964
Hüttl, Ludwig, *Max Emanuel. Der Blaue Kurfürst*, Munich 1976
Schmid, Elmar D., *Nymphenburg*, Munich/London/New York 2000


**Het Loo, Apeldoorn**   page 70

Luikens, Elze, *Apeldoorn in de Schaduw van Het Loo*, Zutphen 1999

# SUGGESTED READING

**Schönbrunn Palace, Vienna**   page 72

Kugler, Georg and Gerhard Trumler, *Schönbrunn*, Vienna 1986
Schmitt, Friedrich, *Schönbrunn Palace*, Schönbrunn 1982
Schwarz, Kurt, *Schönbrunn*, Vienna 1985


**Belvedere Palace, Vienna**   page 74

Mraz, Gottfried, *Prinz Eugen. Ein Leben in Bildern und Dokumenten*, Munich 1985
Mraz, Gottfried and Helmut Nemec, *Belvedere. Schloß und Park des Prinzen Eugen*, Vienna 1988
Oppenheimer, Wolfgang, *Prinz Eugen of Savoyen.* Munich 1996


**Buckingham Palace, London**   page 76

Fontane, Theodor, *A Summer in London*, 1854
Harris, John, et al. (Ed.), *Buckingham Palace and its Treasures*, London 1968
Nash, Roy, *Buckingham Palace. The Palace and the People*, London 1980
Schubert, Ludwig and Rolf Seelmann-Eggebrecht, *Majesty Elisabeth II*, Cologne 2002


**The Zwinger, Dresden**   page 78

Löffler, Fritz, *Der Zwinger in Dresden*, Lipsia 1976
Man, John, *Zwinger Palace*, London 1990
Milde, Kurt, et al. (Ed.), *Daniel Pöppelmann und die Architektur der Zeit Augusts des Starken*, Dresden 1990


**Catherine's Palace, near St. Petersburg**   page 80

Lemus, Vera and Ljudmilla Lapina, *The Palaces and Parks in Pushkin: A Guide*, Moscow 1985
Massie, Robert K., *Last Courts of Europe: A Royal Family Album 1860–1914*, New York 1983


**The Würzburg Residence, Würzburg**   page 82

Bachmann, Erich and Burkard von Roda, *Würzburg Residence and Court Gardens: Official Guide*, Munich 1992
Hubala, Erich, *Balthasar Neumann. Seine Kunst zu bauen*, Stuttgart 1987
Krückmann, Peter O. (Ed.), *Residences of the Prince-Bishops in Franconia*, Munich/London/New York 2002


**Esterháza Palace, near Fertöd**   page 84

Bak, Jolán and István Filep, *Fertöd. Esterházy Kastély*, Budapest 1996
Hokky-Sallay, Marianne, *The Esterháza Palace at Fertöd*, Budapest 1979
Szerzo, Katalin, *Haydn et les Esterházy*, Budapest 1991


**Stupinigi, Turin**   page 86

Griseri, Andreina, *La Palazzina di Stupinigi*, Novara 1982
Macco, Michela di (Ed.), *Le Delizie di Stupinigi*, Turin 1997


**Sanssouci, Potsdam**   page 88

Bassewitz, Gert von and Inge Maisch, *Potsdam and Sanssouci*, Hamburg 1995
Giersberg, Hans-Joachim, et al., *Potsdam and Sans Souci*, Dresden 1975
Hattstein, Markus, *Schloß Sanssouci*, Berlin 2002


**Jag Niwas, Udaipur**   page 90

Ganguli, Kalyan Kumar, *Cultural History of Rajasthan*, New Delhi 1983
Kathuria, Ramdev P., *Life in the Courts of Rajasthan During the 18th Century*, New Delhi 1987
Latzke, Hans E., et al., *Rajasthan*, Cologne 1996
Okada, Amina and Suzanne Held, *Rajasthan, A Land of Splendor and Bravery*, Mumbai 2000
Rousselet, Louis, *India and its Native Princes*, London 1876


**Winter Palace, St. Petersburg**   page 92

Bechtolsheim, Hubert von, *St. Petersburg*, Munich/New York 1994
Bunn, T. Davis, *Winter Palace*, Minneapolis 1993
Ducamp, Emmanuel (Ed.), *The Winter Palace*, Saint Petersburg 1995
Waltenberger, Ingobert, *Prince Eugene's Winter Palace*, Vienna 1998


**Wörlitz Palace, Wörlitz**   page 94

Hirsch, Erhard, *Dessau-Wörlitz. Aufklärung und Frühklassik*, Lipsia 1987
Pfeifer, Ingo, *Schloß Wörlitz*, Munich 2000


**Royal Palace, Bangkok**   page 96

Bhamorabutr, Abha, *The Chakri Dynasty*, Bangkok 1983
Loose, Renate, *Bangkok*, Hong Kong/Boston 1996
Naengnoi, Suksri and Michael Freeman, *Palaces of Bangkok. Royal Residences of the Chakri Dynasty*, London 1996
Sternstein, Larry, *Portrait of Bangkok. Essays in Honour of the Bicentennial Capital of Thailand*, Bangkok 1982


**The Royal Pavilion, Brighton**   page 98

Morley, John, *The Making of the Royal Pavilion*, London 1984
Musgrave, Clifford, *Royal Pavilion. An Episode in the Romantic*, London 1961
Nash, John, *Views of the Royal Pavilion*, edited by Gervase Jackson-Stops, revised new edition of the 1827 edition, London 1991
Rutherford, Jessica M. F., "The Great Kitchen in the Royal Pavilion," in: *Country Life*, 14.12.1989


**Palace of the Winds, Jaipur**   page 100

Aubert, Hans-Joachim, *Rajasthan*, Cologne 2001
Okada, Amina and Suzanne Held, *Rajasthan, A Land of Splendor and Bravery*, Mumbai 2000
Rousselet, Louis, *India and its Native Princes*, London 1876
Tod, James, *Annals and Antiquities of Rajasthan*, 2 Vols., Calcutta 1894

**Sultan's Palace, Zanzibar**   page 102

Ruete, Emilie, *An Arabian Princess Between Two Worlds*, Leiden/New York 1993
Ruete, Emilie, *Memoirs of an Arabian Princess from Zanzibar*, Zanzibar 1998


**Pompeianum, Aschaffenburg**   page 104

Nerdinger, Winfried, (Ed.), *Friedrich von Gärtner*, Munich 1992
Von Roda, Burkard, *Aschaffenburg Castle and Pompeiianum*, Munich 1989
Seibert, Peter, Kathrin Jung and Werner Helmberger, *Der Wiederaufbau des Pompejanums in Aschaffenburg*, Munich 2003


**Miramare Castle, near Trieste**   page 106

Marani, Diego, *A Trieste con Svevo*, Milan 2003
McCourt, John, *The Years of Bloom: James Joyce in Trieste 1904-1920*, Madison, Wisconsin 2000
Morris, Jan, *Trieste: and the Meaning of Nowhere*, New York 2001
Svevo, Italo, *Confessions of Zeno*, New York, 1989


**Neuschwanstein Castle, near Füssen**   page 108

Petzel, Michael, *The Castle of Neuschwanstein*, Munich 1970
Spangenberg, Marcus, *The Throne Room in Schloss Neuschwanstein: Ludwig II of Bavaria and his Vision of Divine Right*, Regensburg 1999


**Achilleion, Corfu**   page 110

Dessaix, Robert, *Corfu: A Novel*, Sydney 2001
Durrell, Lawrence, *Prospero's Cell*, New York 1996
Hannigan, Des, *AA Essential Corfu*, 2003
Tennant, Emma, *A House in Corfu*, London 2002


**Montazah Palace, Alexandria**   page 112

Durrell, Lawrence, *The Alexandria Quartet*, New York 1962
Sartorius, Joachim (Ed.), *Alexandria Fata Morgana*, Stuttgart 2001
Stern, Michael, *Farouk*, New York 1965


**Bahia Palace, Marrakech**   page 114

Canetti, Elias, *The Voices of Marrakesh: A Record of a Visit*, New York 1978
Albrecht Cropp, Johann, *Marocco*, Lucerne 1998


**President's Palace, Havana**   page 116

Engels, Hans, *Havana*, Munich/London/New York 1999
Sweezy, Paul M. and Leo Huberman, *Cuba: Anatomy of a Revolution*, New York 1960


**Hearst Castle, San Simeon**   page 118

Carlson, Oliver and Ernest Sutherland Bates, *Hearst. Lord of San Simeon*, New York 1936
Davis, Gray (Ed.), *Hearst Castle*, Sacramento 2001
Procter, Ben, *William Randolph Hearst. The Early Years 1863-1910*, New York 1998

# INDEX

Front jacket: Palace gate, Belvedere Palace, Vienna, see p. 74
Front cover: Belvedere Palace, Vienna, see p. 74
Back jacket: Potala Palace, Lhasa, see p. 62
Page 1: Royal Pavilion, Brighton, see p. 98
Pages 2–3: Jag Niwas, Uidapur, see p. 90
Pages 8–9: Pool d'Apollon, Versailles Palace, see p. 64
Pages 120–121: Detail of wall, Royal Palace, Bangkok, see p. 96

© Prestel Verlag, Munich · Berlin · London · New York, 2003

Prestel Verlag
Königinstrasse 9
80539 Munich
Tel. +49 (89) 38 17 09-0
Fax +49 (89) 38 17 09-35
www.prestel.de

Prestel Publishing Ltd.
4, Bloomsbury Place
London WC1A 2QA
Tel. +44 (020) 7323-5004
Fax +44 (020) 7636-8004

Prestel Publishing
175 Fifth Avenue, Suite 402
New York, N.Y. 10010
Tel. +1 (212) 995-2720
Fax +1 (212) 995-2733
www.prestel.com

The Library of Congress Control Number: 2003108913

The Deutsche Bibliothek holds a record of this publication in the Deutsche
Nationalbibliografie; detailed bibliographical data can be found under:
http://dnb.ddb.de

Prestel books are available worldwide. Please contact your nearest bookseller or
one of the above addresses for information concerning your local distributor.

Translated from the German by John W. Gabriel, Worpswede

Editorial direction by Katharina Haderer
Picture research by Sandra Leitte
Copyedited by Curt Holtz

Design and layout by Ulrike Schmidt
Origination by ReproLine, Munich
Printing by Sellier, Freising
Binding by Conzella, Pfarrkirchen

Printed in Germany on acid-free paper

ISBN 3-7913-2914-6

## Photographic Credits

The author and publisher have gone to great lengths to obtain copyright
clearance for the illustrations in this publication. The author and the
publisher would be pleased to hear from any copyright holder who could
not be traced.

The figures refer to page numbers (t = top, b = bottom, l = left, r = right,
c = center)

Aero Luftbild GmbH 28 b l
akg-images, Berlin, front jacket; 28 t, b r, 58 b, 112 t, Dieter E. Hoppe 29
  b; Pirozzi 31 b; Ruhrgas AG 81 b
allOver, Kleve  Rainer Grosskopf 34 t l; Andree Großkämper 118 t, 119;
  JBE Photo 13 t, b l; Dieter Schinner 72  t l; Tom Weber 118 b l; Heike
  Werner 100 b
artur, Cologne  René Menges 29 t
The Bavarian Administration of State Castles and Palaces, Gardens and
  Lakes, Munich  69 b l, 104 b l, 105
Lothar Beckel, Salzburg  19 b
Achim Bednorz, Cologne  18 b, 20 b l, 56/57, 73, 75 b r, 78 t, 86 b, 87
Helga Bemmann, *Kurt Tucholsky. Ein Lebensbild*, Berlin 1990 48 l
Bilderberg, Hamburg  C. Boisvieux 114 b l
Christoph & Friends, Essen  Friedrich Stark 103 b
Corbis, Düsseldorf  Michael S. Yamashita 59 b
Axel Griesinger  61 t
Bildagentur Anne Hamann  Wilfried Bauer 92 b l
Heinrich Harrer, *Erinnerungen an Tibet*, Frankfurt am Main/Berlin 1993
  62 r
Oswald Hederer, *Friedrich von Gärtner 1792–1847* Munich 1976  104 t
Markus Hilbich, Berlin  15 b r, 25 t, b, 31 t, 52 b l
Historischer Verein Neuburg, Schloß Neuburg  52 t r
Bildagentur Huber, Garmisch-Partenkirchen  27 t, 52 b r, 61 b, 65 t, b l
  (and 8/9); F. Damm 98/99; Fantuz 74 t l (and front cover); Giovanni
  60 b, 94 b, 95 b; Gräfenhain 55 t, 66/67, 67 b r, 80 t; Ripani 76 t;
  B. Römmelt 68/69; R. Schmid 19 t, 35, 45 t, 117 t
Hungarian National Office of Cultural Heritage  85 b
IFA, Munich  Aberham 91 b, 101 t, b; Barnes 50/51; Diaf 65 b r; Fried
  62 c l; P. Graf 96/97; Harris 22 b l; Hasenkopf 53; Hunter 96 t (and
  120/121); IT/tpl 16/17; Jochem 49 t; Kneer 81 t; Kneuer 115 b; Birgit
  Koch 91 t (and 2/3); Kohlhas 111 b l; Lescourret 47 t, b; R. Maier 84 t;
  Neupert-Christians 72 b l; NOK-Photo 13 b r, 96 b r, 109; W. Otto 94 t
  l, 110/111; Rölle 39 b; Russia 37 t, 93; Fritz Schmid 1, 98 t (and 1);
  Siebig 33 t; Simanor 21, 62 t l; TPC 41 b r, 59 t, 100 t l; Tschanz 85 t
*Die königlichen Schlösser in Großbritannien*, Munich 1991 38 b l, 76 b
*Der königliche Pavillon*, Brighton 1995 98 b, 99 b
laif, Cologne  Celentano 107 t, b r; Emmler 112/113, 113 b r; Gaasterland
  33 b r; Paul Hahn 18 t; Andreas Hub 83, 108 b r; Manfred Linke 43 b r;
  Modrow 90 b, 96 b l; Anna Neumann 23; Heiko Specht 114 b r;
  Tophoven 34 b; Paul Trummer 111 b r; F. Zanettini 77 t
Nancy E. Loe, *William Randolph Hearst. An Illustrated Biography*, Santa
  Barbara 1988 118 b r
LOOK, Munich  Hauke Dressler 49 b, 88 b l, 103 t; Christian Heeb 77 b;
  Karl Johaentges 27 b l; Kay Maeritz 63 (and back cover); Jürgen Richter
  79 t; Florian Werner 108 t; Heinz Wohner 88 t; Konrad Wothe 27 b r
Bildarchiv Monheim, Meerbusch  Lisa Hammel/Annet van der Voort 14 b
Florian Monheim  20 b r, 40/41, 42 t, 43 t, b l, 55 b l, b r, 69 b r, 71 b l,
  b r, 72 b c, 75 t, 79 b, 82 b, 92 b r, 95 t; Florian Monheim/Roman von
  Götz 89
Werner Neumeister, Munich  15 t, 22 t, 39 t, 108 b l
Paul den Boer, *The Royal Palace Noordeinde in an Historical View*, Zutphen
  1986 45 b r
Archivio Scala, Florence (Antella)  33 b l, 46 t
Klaus Staps  104 b r
Martin Thomas  117 b r
WFVV  75 b l
Thomas Peter Widmann, Regensburg  115 t
Ernst Wrba, Sulzbach am Taunus  70 b, 71 t
Zeitenspiegel, Weinstadt  Roberto Salas 117 b l